The Dance of Life

Invitation to A
Father-Daughter Dance

B.J. Funk

Dedication

To all women everywhere
Who long to dance;

And to the memory of my parents,
Nell and J.C. Greene,

Who danced in marriage for sixty-two years.

Acknowledgements

I am grateful to my sister, Beverly Hickox, a retired high school English teacher and the best line-by-line editor I know. She lovingly handled my manuscript to make sure the end project gave the message I wanted. As she read, she encouraged me and made me believe in myself and in my purpose for this book. She has always done that for me, though. Her belief in me has undergirded everything I have ever done. Three years older than me and my only sibling, Beverly's view of me as her little sister has never changed. She would still fight anybody who hurt me. In fact, we've always been the other's biggest supporter. Working with her as my editor has been a great joy and privilege.

I am grateful to my dear friend, Susan Terry, who moved with me through each chapter of this manuscript and gave me her gift of making a paragraph better and tighter. Susan spent many hours reading my work. I trusted her insights spiritually as well as her ability to offer the reader a stronger and clearer presentation of my work. I took every suggestion she gave, because I had great confidence in her desire to be part of helping women know God personally. Besides, she is a lot of fun. We laughed and worked, and she gave me, as she always does, some treasured memories.

I am grateful to my husband of nearly 24 years, Roy Funk. He believes in my call to ministry. If I have not had time to clean the house, he picks up the dust mop and does it himself. He cooks most of our meals so that I can make visits to the hospital and do other work of ministry. I stay in front of the computer a lot, and he never complains. His support is a daily gift that I treasure.

Table of Contents

Introduction

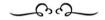

Have you ever wondered why so many women are hurting? Why do they feel incomplete? Why does guilt keep them from living productive lives? Why do they think God is mad at them? The answer to their misery is right before them. It's resting in the outstretched arms of Jesus at Calvary. We have heard about this all of our lives; yet the truth of this love story often escapes us. We don't understand. How can God love us that much? Why is His death connected to our lives and to our feeling of completeness? I hope you will find some answers to these questions in this book and that you will hear his heart of love for you personally through these chapters.

This book is about a dance. There are two main characters. One is you. The other is your Father God. It is the story of His desire to bring you into His Dance, showing you possibilities for your life that you never imagined. It is the story of His Love, an amazing love that transcends human understanding.

It is the story of your real Father, Father God, your Heavenly Father. It is a story of His desire to bring you through the storms of life and into the safety of His robe. He wants to walk beside you, helping you when life seems more than you can handle. He wants to help you move past any relationships that hurt you, defeat you, control you or abuse you. He wants you to understand the depth of love He has for you. His love soothes and settles the broken places in your heart. His love revives all that has been stolen from you. He has a plan for your life. You will find that plan in the pages of this book.

The Dance of Life is primarily about your Father, but because you are His daughter, the book will also be about you. The two of you are joined, and so a story about Him must include a story about you. In this book, you will learn that your Father God views you with eyes of love and compassion. You will learn that He treats you with consideration and respect.

To grasp the full meaning of God's love, you will need to view Him as a God who is *alive*. He has a throne in heaven where He sits and watches over the world. He also came to earth in the form of His Son Jesus Christ, who was murdered and then arose from the dead. God is alive. He is not a far away, unreachable, untouchable God. He is a thinking, acting, interacting Being. He speaks. He listens. He hears. And He is always ready to stop making a new cloud or bursting through the hard ground with a new flower if you, His daughter, need Him. He knows the intricate workings of your physical and spiritual self because He made you. He has a reason He wanted you on this earth.

He is a Father who wants to teach you what a Father's love is like. Maybe you have some understanding of that from the earthly father you were given. Maybe you don't. He is too well aware that you have pain in your life, and He sees His Father role as being the One to comfort you from one hour to the next. He has this giant shoulder that has been used by many of his children. Paul put His head on it. David did. Naomi did. Noah did. All of these had problems they did not know how to solve. Your Father's shoulder is well padded and used. When you rest your head on His shoulder, you are resting it in good company. You are lying where others lay who grew strength from their Father and had the courage to keep on going. It doesn't hurt that when you put your head there, His great big arm of love enfolds you.

God views you with holy eyes. He sees your immense possibilities. He treasures your femininity. He cherishes your tender heart. He protects your vulnerability. He treats you like a lady.

Your Father God is constantly busy in your behalf, and as Isaiah states in chapter 49:16, *God has you engraved on the palm of his hands*! Whatever He does today, whenever He turns His hand to create a new miracle, there it is! Your name! Right on His palm. He looks at your name and is reminded of how very much you mean to Him. He constantly tries to whisper the truth of His faithfulness into your ears.

Deuteronomy 33:26 describes Him this way. "There is none like God, who rides on the clouds to help you…." This Father loves you enough to stop everything else He is doing, jump into His chariot, and use His fastest moving winds to propel Him right to you and your need. He would do this just so He can get to you and help you.

God's view of you is completely different from what you may have thought of yourself. He wants to pull you into this love relationship by loving you and validating your existence. He sees your gifts and graces. He knows about your unrecognized talents. He knows about the potential buried under layers and layers of pain. He is the only one who can move you out of days of despair. He can heal your wounds and transform your scars.

He is the CEO of heaven, with many unprecedented successes. He is the King of the Universe, mighty in power with the ability to rain down torrents of disaster with just the blink of His eye. His tender nature always prevails. Justice is one of His Names; yet, Mercy is the sign He chooses to hang on His wall.

Because no earthly relationship can ever match the relationship that your Father offers, you might have to "unlearn" some things you associate with the word *father*. In this book, you are asked to go beyond the confined realm of earth and move into heavenly places. You are asked to allow your Father to heal the pain of your heart, that pain placed there by earthly disappointments. You will be asked to imagine your Father God as a Friend with whom you can talk, a

Confidant whom you can trust, and a Father with whom you can communicate.

You will be asked to take His hand and move on to the Dance Floor of Life, where His plans are always good. You will be asked to take the first step in faith, allowing His love to flow all over you as you continue the Dance. His heart sees your hesitancy, feels your pulling away, but He persists. He comes to you as a wooing Lover, always urging you forward, always helping you to reach for those goals He has for you. If you will take His hand and move into the Dance, you will like the person you become. That person will be who God intended you to be in the first place. Chains will drop. Past pain will be lessened, but in order to find these freedoms, you have to continue the Dance.

The real story of the way your Heavenly Father views you is written in these next chapters. Before you read the first one, remind yourself this book will be an experience of faith. You will want to purposefully ask Him to remove any preconceived ideas about Him, some put there by negative influences in your life as well as those that came to you just because of your own assumptions. God is not out to hurt you, upset you, misuse you or abuse you. He is all about Love. Maybe that is a new concept for you. You have thought of Him only as Judge. You have seen Him as a Creator who made a mistake when He made you. You have resented what you felt were His interruptions in your life. You've held anger against Him because things haven't always worked out the way you wanted. You don't understand His ways, so you stopped trying to find His heart.

God usually gets the bad press for what others have done to us, especially when trust has been broken. We unfairly place God in the same category with fallen mankind, assuming that He can't be trusted either. If the blueprint of your life has not turned out like you wanted, and if your view of God has been blurred through earthly pain and misunderstanding, God wants a chance to show you another way of thinking.

In this book, you will find His love dancing through every thought, between the spaces of the words and in the margins. You will hear Him calling out to you, bringing you in to His Dance of Life with every sentence. Hopefully, you will hear His true heart, the heart of a Father for his child.

This book will give you information you might never have heard, things that teach you how a good, loving Father feels about His daughter! It is for young, middle-aged and older daughters. The purpose is to help you realize how much God loves you and to refocus any negative views of God into positive ones. Hopefully, you will come to recognize the unfailing, incredible, redeeming and personal love of your Heavenly Father.

Perhaps you walk in bondage today because you have not allowed God to hold you on His lap as your Father, walk by you in faithfulness as your mate, and stick by you closer than any brother or step brother. Sadly, you might never have allowed His grace to melt your own steel box of pain.

God sees you through *forgiveness lens* that wipe away your shortcomings. He cleans your life with fresh waters of never-ending love. He has good plans for you, but before you can begin to walk in those plans, you must understand that you are His very special daughter, a delight to His heart! While God does long to walk beside you, husband you, protect and befriend you, He includes all of those attributes and more as your Father.

Pray before you read the first chapter. Ask the Holy Spirit to open your heart to begin to receive a new way of thinking about God. If you're not sure how to pray, I'd like to offer a suggestion.

Prayer: Dear God, I read in the Bible where you are all about love, but sometimes life gets in my way and I push you aside. I desire to know you in a new way. Please help me. Clean out my cobwebs of past memories, hurtful words, and unmet needs. Sweep my mind clean as You begin a new understanding within me. I really want to understand your love. I want to know what it means to be your daughter. AMEN.

Chapter One

The Father-Daughter Dance

On the day you were conceived in your Mother's womb, God took out His heavenly diary and began writing in detailed form His carefully thought-out plan concerning you. He had known about this plan since before time began, but now that you would actually be a living, breathing person in just nine short months, He wanted to make sure He had covered every little detail. His heart must have jumped with delight as He thought about you and about the joy the two of you could share. In His diary, His words went something like this:

"Dear Diary, I have many dreams for this precious life now being formed. I want so much for her to be filled with joy, happiness and completeness. I want her to know my deep love for her!"

He went on to write down certain people and circumstances that He would use, all orchestrated by a carefully thought out plan, divine in origin and vibrating with the love of the Father's heartbeat. He continued to write.

"Is it so strange that I, the Creator of this child, would want to know her love? Is it so strange that I, her Maker, would long for her to run to me with her problems? Is it not understandable that I want to be there for her? I want to hold her when she's hurting, and I want to bear her burdens."

And then, as God began to write the next sentence, all of heaven stood still; indeed heaven could feel His intense concern, His deep desire. His words echoed off the Pearly Gates and into the silence of the angels, shaking heaven's floor as God finished His sentence with an exclamation mark!

"I want," the Father wrote, "Oh, how I want *a relationship* with this child. Not that she would just hear about me, or think about me every now and then, or call on me just when she's hurting. I want her to receive my love and love me back. I will offer her not just a relationship, but also a covenant relationship, one that is solid and true, binding and trustworthy. I want her to know me as her best friend, and I in turn, will burst with joy over the delight she will bring to my heart."

Then, in outline form, He arranged His plan, a plan that would get your attention, one that would bring you to the point where you would want to receive this sweet and satisfying relationship with Him. He entered number one.

(1) Love her into knowing Me!
    He entered number two of His plan.
(2) Love her into knowing Me!
    And, last, He entered number three.
(3) Love her into knowing Me!

And with that, He closed His diary. And nine months later, when you were born, God began a heavenly courtship with you, a divine romance of love, with the intention of bringing you into His heart and into a loving, satisfying relationship with Him.

On the morning of your birth, God was almost giggly! He scribbled love messages and drew hearts all over the birth announcement He sent to the angels! The children's choir sang "Rock A Bye Baby" over and over again, way past their bedtime. Every heavenly being congratulated God. He was a Father again, and He loved it! His helpers tied pink bows on every star and put your picture on heaven's bulletin board, with your weight and footprint underneath. If heaven hadn't had a No Smoking policy, God probably would have passed out cigars!

As you grew older, He viewed each detail with delightful anticipation! When your first tooth arrived, He beamed. When you started walking, He wrote the news on heaven's doorposts. When you fell down and cried, He hurt, too. He watched you take off on your first bicycle, holding His breath until you made it safely down the driveway. When you started school, He held His head up a little higher. A proud Dad!

From time to time, He would write in His diary His joy in knowing you. He could hardly wait until you would trust Him to lead you through the Dance of Life.

As the years grew, He watched when your first boyfriend jilted you and left you for another. Realizing this was a part of growing up, He bowed His head in grief as you cried, longing to run to your side. God watched you through the years as other heartaches and rejections came your way. Each time, He moved closer to you, reaching out to you to let you know He cared. Sometimes, you were hurting too much to even notice. He longed to shield you from hurt. He wanted to hold you when you were in pain. Often, He cried.

When I was in my forties, my daddy had a stroke. He would never walk again. One day, he cried as he said to me, "Last night I dreamed you were in a wreck, and you needed me. I couldn't get to you." There was agony in his voice and pain all over his face. He realized his dream was all too true. He would not have been able to come help me. His own disability took a backseat to his intense longing to be a father who could help his daughter when she needed him.

Your heavenly Father feels that way, too. He wants to come when you need Him. He is an actively present, living God, yet He lives in the spiritual realm. Though He's not handicapped, as my father was, He usually chooses not to move through the restraints of gravity, laws of nature, human will, or man's inhumanity to man. If He operated that way, we would have seen Him riding in as a knight in shining armor to rescue his Son from the cruelty of man. He would have stepped in to save a man named Stephen from being stoned to death.

Because of a love so great we cannot even begin to fathom it, God steps back in order to allow mankind to swim in his own river of self- destruction. He knows we are stubborn and rebellious. He also knows that our willful ways lead to no good and yet will be a part of what He can use to draw us to His side. He knows us so well. It is only when we are in a fire that we go looking for a fireman. When we turn to Him, He is there to save us and pull us to safety.

Never think that God writes a fresh pain on a new baseball, taking great pleasure as He throws it straight at you! That's not what our Father God is like. That's what the Evil One is like. God is a Father filled with mercy, compassion, and love. He never means for you to be hurt. His original plan was for you to live with Him forever in His first created garden.

During the bad times and the good times of your life, your Heavenly Father watches. Because He knows everything that the Adversary is planning to throw at you, He's not asleep when that wretched snake makes his evil moves! In a way hard to grasp with our limited understanding, your Father takes those hurts in your life and starts working everything together for your *good!* While the enemy is jumping up and down and shouting "Yippee" over his temporary win to hurt you, God is working out minute by minute explicit details for your complete care.

We have the picture all wrong. It's not that Satan strikes, and God then goes to work. It's that God is already at work when Satan strikes! God saw it coming, and He is stronger, higher, and more capable than anything Satan can throw at you! Oswald Chambers says that God uses even the Adversary for His own purposes. (*My Utmost For His Highest,* Oswald Chambers, Dodd, Mead and Company, New York, 1935) God's plan all along was to love you into knowing Him, and He uses everything He can find to make sure you know that!

Being the wise Father He is, and having learned on so many previous children, He gives you opportunity to explore your world and make choices. He doesn't like the heartache that comes with those choices any more than you do, but He will not take away your freedom to choose. He hovers nearby though, formulating love plans, putting notes in His diary, and checking with your guardian angel on your progress. All the while, He sends love messages to you. Sometimes you notice; other times you don't.

There are those times when He is so close to you that, if you stop to listen, you can hear His heartbeat! God joins you on every joyful moment, bursting with pride just because you are His! He also joins you in every disappointing moment, and when it is over and you come out okay, you may not even realize it was because of Him. That's okay. He isn't looking for a pat on the back; He's just looking for ways to show you His love.

He's not interested in how much money you have, how you dress, or even how you act, as far as loving you is concerned. He is not going to change His mind about you! He's in for the long haul, thoroughly committed to you! You are His daughter, the delight of His heart, the apple of His eye! He wants a relationship with you. His heart is always tuned in to yours. All He asks back from you is your love.

For some reason, that's the hardest thing to give. Why? Because giving our love to Him exposes our extreme devotion to ourselves, cutting us with words like submission, obedience, dying to self and giving our all. We don't like those words! They hit us in the stomach with reality! They bite! They cause us to see ourselves naked, without our clothes of pride. They expose our worst parts and open up memories we wanted to bury. We become vulnerable and defensive.

At these times, your Father comes to you and gently opens old wounds and hurts, memories and bruises. Lovingly, and with the touch of a master, He loves each pain with His kiss, holding you in His lap all the while.

He is your Abba Father! You are His Princess Adorable! He has all the time in the world for you and your concerns. He always has His ears tuned to listen to your problems, and He longs to guide you into successful answers. He wants you to be content and full of joy. He would go to any extreme to bring you into this close relationship with Him. In fact, He already did.

He came to earth as a baby, walked the dusty roads of Galilee teaching, preaching and healing. All the time, He was thinking about YOU! Though you weren't even born, your name was engraved on his palm. As He moved from town to town and saw evil's pull, He wanted to make this world a better place for you. Knowing that there was only one way to make the world safe, He climbed on a cross and endured tremendous pain so that you could know freedom from the bondage of sin. He endured the agony of an unbearable death so that you would be free to tell Satan to stuff it! He came back from death so that you wouldn't be afraid to die. He is your biggest hero! He conquered death, sin and fear for you!

On that morning when He arose, He sat up and looked around the empty tomb. His eyes immediately looked at His palm. Ah! Your name! Still there! Even the nails couldn't destroy the engraving! He thrilled with the realization that sin could never lock you in chains! You would be free! He looked up into the heavens and breathed deeply.

His daughter, YOU, would never have to be afraid of the tomb! Because your Father had been there before you and conquered all fear, you could move with great freedom and assurance in your life and into your death. He never wanted you to be afraid.

Your Father God doesn't just care about you. He adores you. He's your biggest fan. He waits up at night for you to come home. He watches out for you every hour of the day, and He never goes to bed. If He had a Christmas tree, He would want you to be the only gift underneath. You would be enough! Even when you get angry with His ways, He doesn't walk away. He stays.

All throughout your life, your Father God has been calling you into a love relationship with Him. Have you heard His heart concerning you? Are you listening to His voice calling you to come closer? He desires nothing more than for you to walk and talk daily with Him.

Your Father God wants to provide everything you need! After all, He owns everything. You've even been written into His will! Guess what? He has left it all to you!

No matter what earth's circumstances have handed you, or what people's circumstances have caused you, your Father God has not let you go. He will continue pursuing you and wooing you and loving you until you say YES to His heart's desire. He wants to love you into loving Him back! He wants a relationship with you!

Every day of your life from this time on can be a new walk with your Father. His love is warm and real, exciting and refreshing. It's like getting chocolate candy when you didn't even ask; like receiving a bouquet of fresh flowers you didn't expect; like finding a valentine in your mailbox in July; like opening a gift when your birthday has already passed. It's like feeling safe and secure just when you thought your boat was about to capsize.

God's love pulls you to Him and places His arms around you. Soon, you begin to recognize those loving arms as you slowly sway in a rhythm of His love. Hourly, daily and forever the love walk with you continues. It's like a dance, a Father-Daughter Dance.

Ever been to one? Usually, they occur around Valentine's Day at Primary Schools where children five to nine aren't embarrassed to dance with their father! In fact, they love it! They don't say, "I don't deserve this dance! I'll stand in line and let everybody else dance with my father first!"

On the contrary, they want *no one else* to dance with their father! They love to be with him in that endearing and wonderful way. They love to be close to him.

In the same way, we must not say, "I don't deserve this dance with my heavenly Father. I've done too many things wrong." When two people get out on the dance floor, neither goes according to their list of virtuous living. They go because that's where they want to be.

This life is *your* dance, and you only get one chance at it. God stands waiting as your willing partner on the dance floor. You don't have to live a life of less than your best! You were made for a reason, and God wants you to find that reason. It is a simple one. *You are made to be in a right relationship with your Father God through His Son, Jesus Christ.* Hopefully, through reading this book, you will come to understand this reason even better.

Get caught up in His arms and listen to the music. Let Him hold you close and lead, as you follow. He will move into the right places on the dance floor. In fact, you can trust Him to listen to your concerns as you sway together. Just being in His arms brings such joy and peace.

Begin to learn about this Father who loves you this much! If you will let Him, He will dance with you throughout each day of your life, loving you into a satisfying and blessed relationship with Him.

Life is a dance. Everyone knows it's no fun to dance alone. You need a partner!

You don't know how to dance? Come on. Walk on the dance floor. He will take your hand and be your instructor from now until forever. Can you hear the music? It's the music for the Father-Daughter Dance! Don't be shy. He's waiting.

To My Reader: You probably aren't used to hearing God's love for you described this way. These words may be very new for you; perhaps they are a little uncomfortable. Stay with me. Believe it. His love for you is strong and true and never leaves. He is looking forward to your getting to know Him better through the pages of this book. I would like to pray that He helps you as you search for this love relationship with your Father.

Prayer: Dear Father, you are important enough to me that I want to believe what I am reading. I want to believe you love me this much, but you know the pain in my life. You know how hard life has been for me some times. You know my struggles for approval, my insecurities. Love me into knowing you as I go through this book. I want to know you better. In Jesus' name I pray, Amen.

Chapter Two

May I Have This Dance?

When your Father God created you, He wrote a personal love invitation, and sewed it into your heart. He used pink thread that would never wear out no matter how old you became. Whatever you are doing and wherever you go, in all the circumstances of your life, your Father God wants you to remember what His invitation says.

Written in bold letters of love are these words, now safely resting inside of you as they have been from the minute you were created.

"Dear Daughter, You are my dream girl! You have stolen my heart! Everything about you is beautiful to me! I am planning a lifetime ball in your honor. Join me on a forever waltz of love. I'm waiting. I love you, Your Father."

The invitation is warm and appealing, but you are hesitant. Is this really what God says to you? How can you partake in the celebration of this invitation when you know too well that you don't deserve a ball in your honor. After all, the very first day you were on earth, you began a rebellion. You cried as loudly as you could, kept your mother up half the night, screamed when you got hungry, and pitched a fit when someone wouldn't hold you. You did nothing to deserve an invitation to God's ball, and yet He invited you anyway, even before your head was in the birth canal!

As you grew older, you learned the ways of the world all too well. Perhaps you became a cunning manipulator or a skillful controller. You looked in the mirror and decided that everything needed to revolve around you. Maybe your parents gave you that message; maybe they didn't. No matter. You knew the truth anyway. You were adorable, cute, funny and lovable and in your mind, everything else should stop at your command. You whined when your mother was on the phone, threw your toys when you got mad, and pouted when people didn't do what you wanted them to do. While you may have been quite compelling in your adorable little girl ways, you learned early in life how to call the shots. The only salvation to your demands came if you had solid, consistent parents who were more determined than you. They held out to say "No" when necessary, put you in your room to cool off, and even used good old fashioned discipline to teach you that no matter how hard you tried, you really weren't the boss.

I am so thankful for my parents' loving, yet firm, discipline. Somewhere in my high school days, I realized that boundaries set by my earthly father were not only a safety net for me; they also spared me the repercussions from bad choices, thus taking away any unnecessary pressure. I didn't have to decide what time I came in from a date. My father set that time. I didn't have to decide if I should go to certain events. My father made that decision for me. Rather than stripping me of my ability to determine right from wrong, his guidelines served as a predetermined comfort zone. I rested in his wisdom while I was in our home. Instead of viewing his parenting as that of a warden, I saw him more as a guardian, a keeper, a shield.

My father had no trouble expressing his views on how to bring up my older sister and me. There were no arguments in our home about late dates, excessive spending, talking back, or disrespect. Those things didn't happen because he mixed great love with his discipline. Like a valued watchman, my father walked beside us as an escort rather than before us like a dictator. He always hugged us after he corrected us. We never doubted that he loved us.

That's how our Father God is. He wants to be our escort, not our dictator. He never intended for us to manage our lives on our own, without Him. He never wanted us to try to find our own way without any Fatherly guidance. He wants to show us the security of His plan for our lives, and He longs to walk beside us on our earthly journey.

One of my favorite hymns is "I Come To the Garden Alone." When I think of that hymn, I can almost jump right into the middle of that garden and literally smell the roses. In the early morning dew, I sense someone else walking with me, and am over-joyed to know that it is my Father God! The writer states in the chorus, *He walks with me and He talks with me, and He tells me I am his own!*

Do you hear those words? First of all, God wants to walk with you, His daughter! It's natural that a loving Father wants to spend time with His daughter! The two of you make a treasured picture, walking in a lovely garden, just as the dew is falling, and the sun is rising. What a beautiful revelation of His love! The unbelievable part of those words is the hidden message that God chooses to come into the garden with you! He doesn't have to come. He could choose to do anything else He wanted to do, but He chooses to be with you! He doesn't walk ahead of you or behind you, but right beside you. He walks *with you*.

However, He doesn't settle only for walking in the garden with you. He talks with you in the garden. He doesn't look away from you as He talks. He doesn't carry a newspaper under his arm, pulling it out to scan the headlines as He talks with you. He doesn't use demeaning words or argumentative statements. He doesn't scream or yell. He *talks* with you. Maybe some of your family or friends have talked harshly to you, cut you down with overpowering words, intimidated you with their sarcasm, taken advantage of you with their words, or walked beside you with the silent treatment, not talking at all!

But your Father God *talks!* The wonderful Creator of heaven and earth chooses to talk, and He chooses to talk to you! You can take great comfort today in that fact. He actually enjoys your company! He chooses to meet you in the garden for an early morning chat! He has nothing better on his mind, no list to check off, no job to report to, no chores to finish. He just comes to walk and talk with you. That's incredibly refreshing news if you have felt nobody else really wants to talk to you at all.

If someone chooses to talk to you, then they are choosing to be your friend. You might be surprised to know that your Father God wants to actually be a friend. I hope you can begin to comprehend Father and friend being used to identify the same person. Your Father God *knows* how to be your friend! He knows how to love you the way a dear friend loves you. He is God Almighty, your Creator. He placed the desire inside of you for friendship. Until you allow Him to fill that pre-ordained spot with Himself, you will be unable to reach the potential God has planned for you.

The next part in the chorus of *In the Garden* comes after the writer tells you that God walks and talks with you. Then you learn what God tells you in the garden. Get ready. It's amazing and creative, and yet unbelievably simple! He tells you that *you* belong to Him. The words are "He walks with me and talks with me, and He tells me *I am His own*."

I can think of nothing sweeter than to know that our Father God whispers those words to you and me. We are His! His invitation to the Ball remains despite what we were doing before we got to the garden that morning. The invitation remains no matter how badly we messed up the night before! His invitation remains even if we've never sent a RSVP! Sewn inside your heart and mine, the invitation remains. We belong to Him, and He wants us in His presence.

The rest of that chorus puts the finishing touch on the excitement of your time with Him in the garden. *The joy we share as we tarry there, none other has ever known!* There is JOY for you as you remain in the garden with your Father. There is a joy that is so sweet that it would seem no one else on earth could possibly know anything about it. That joy is too compelling to describe, too beautiful to paint, too wonderful to even write about. We can't really find the right words. It is a joy that doesn't fit into your mind's limited understanding. It is pure tranquility and total harmony with God's plan for you! That joy is deep rest and blessed contentment. With joy like that residing in you, what can possibly pull you away? Why would you ever want to leave a garden like that?

And yet you must. The eight o'clock job calls out to you, and the children's carpool is waiting. Groceries can't get into the pantry without you, and neither will the dishes wash themselves. For all the joy of being in solitude with your Father God, the weight of the world constantly battles its own cry for attention. Still, He doesn't pull the invitation, even when you walk away. That remains, along with His devoted eyes of love following you throughout the many demands of your busy life.

Perhaps this description of a devoted Father who loves you and wants to spend time with you is too difficult for you to comprehend. God meant for you to be revered, honored and loved. But, the enemy has taken many women's minds captive to his lies. Your Enemy, the Evil One, wants you to view your heavenly Father the same way you view your earthly father, your grandfather, your husband or any other man who has ever stripped you of the dignity and worth you deserve. Those men who have hurt you and robbed you of this joyful understanding of a heavenly Father are men who never considered God's plan for you as a woman. They never saw your sacred worth and the invaluable contributions you could give to this world. For whatever reason, they couldn't give to you; instead they took, and what they took has cut into your soul daily like a sharp knife. One or more of them might have convinced you that you were of little use to anyone, and that you would never amount to anything. What is it about us as women? We tend to actually *believe* those things that are told us over and over. We come to view ourselves in the exact same way as we are treated.

Maybe nothing was spoken, but perhaps a negative attitude was conveyed. It didn't take you long to realize you weren't wanted, you were in the way, and that what you thought didn't matter. It didn't take you long to stop recognizing the tremendous worth of you. In fact, if you have lived much of your life hiding behind your excuses for those men's actions, defending them in order to keep peace, you have lost so much of yourself that you likely cannot even recognize your great loss. Somewhere in between the verbal, physical or sexual abuse, a beautiful daughter of God learned how to play man's game so that she survived from day to day. Survival, however, was in outward appearances only. Inwardly, there was death.

The men who damaged you had strong personalities or charming abilities. Because you could see and hear them, what they said seemed to make sense. Besides, maybe they were right. Maybe you were what they said you were. Not much to look at. No fun to be with. Not worth the price of your next meal. Terrible, terrible injustices have been falsely sent into women's hearts and minds by overbearing men whose actions clearly showed that they had no respect at all for one of God's brightest creations.

When you were a child, you had little control over what happened to you at the hands of an unloving man. But, as an adult, you do. Imbedded in your heart's pain are those negative memories, but your Father God wants to tell you something. He wants to tell you that you are not what you have been led to believe. Your negative image of yourself is not your true self. The grandest possibilities are in you. There are great achievements waiting to happen, a lot of love to give, and avenues of grace that have been road-blocked all of your life.

All the while, your Father God kept calling your name, trying to show you His invitation. "It's right there," he whispered. "Right there in your heart. I put it there. It will always be there. I love you."

In your lowest moments, God sends His sweet offer of hope. He wants you to come away with Him to a Dance of Life. He desires to hold you as His daughter and to bring you onto His dance floor. He wants you to believe in His love for you! He is tired of the way you have been treated and what Satan has done to you! He yearns for you to see yourself in His mirror of acceptance. As you move busily throughout each day, searching for meaning, trying new remedies, and falling back into the same patterns of defeat, He wants you to stop and listen to Him. What He desires you to hear are these words.

"Trust me. Come to me. I can take care of all those hurts. I will hold you and love you as we move through your days together. Don't keep trying to do it all by yourself. Stop running from me. I would never hurt you, betray you or leave you. I'm staying right here on life's dance floor with you. I want to offer you the warmth of my embrace, the security of my arms, the joy of knowing me as your Father. Come to me, my love. May I have this dance?"

Only a God dedicated to faithfulness would continue to stay past continual rejections. Your Father God is like that. He will not push you or make you come. He wants to love you into knowing Him, and He can wait. You're worth waiting for!

Once you come to Him and allow Him to hold you in a continual embrace of love, you will never be satisfied again with less. You may decide to break away from the music of His dance and run back to your old ways, but his devotion for you will never stop. He will be standing in the middle of the dance floor long after everyone else has left, and the band has gone home.

You will find Him waiting. Waiting to dance with you again.

To My Reader: Did you know there is a place in your heart reserved just for your Father God? Nothing else can adequately fill that place. Your Father longs to take you to the Dance of Life and show you how much He cares about you. Has today been a terribly difficult day for you? Has the week been an onslaught of negatives? Your Father calls you to a friendship with Him. He wants to walk and talk with you. Will you let Him? May I pray with you for that to happen?

Prayer: My Father, I've never thought you would like to be my friend. I've never thought of your love reaching into my heart in such a way that you walk with me and talk with me. I always thought of you as way up there, higher than my spirit could ever reach. I don't understand this, but I want it. I want an intimate day-by-day walk with you. I want to hear you talking to me each day. Please help me. Thank you. In your Son's Name, Amen.

Chapter Three

A Corsage For You

Will you look with me at the story of creation? What was Eve thinking? When tempted to eat the enticing fruit, she acted alone. Adam was not standing nearby saying, "Well, I will if you will, but you go first." When Satan tempted Eve, she did not turn around and say, "Adam, should I?" Instead, she listened to the snake, and what he said made a lot of sense to her untrained and undisciplined mind. The snake told Eve that she would not die, as God had warned, if she ate the fruit. Instead, things would only get better. She would possess the same vision and wisdom that God had. What she knew of God, however, was limited. She only knew Him as Creator, not as Savior, Redeemer, Best Friend and Helper, and she loved the idea of standing on center stage and being co-powerful with Him.

Satan told her also that she would know the difference between good and evil. Eve had not been to school, nor brought up by a mother and father, so one would think Eve might have asked, "What does good mean? What is evil?" She must have decided that knowing the difference between the two, whatever they meant, must be great! She bit the lie, took the bait, and then went over to reel Adam in.

She had only recently been made, of course, arriving in the garden as a grown woman and completely skipping childhood, puberty and youth. Eve had not been a person long when she decided that her good brain and thinking process, one of God's generous gifts to her on the day she was created, could just take a back seat. If God had allowed her to have monthly cramps first, without the invention of heating pads or Mydol, she might have thought twice before disobeying Him. She might have thought, "If my disobedience is going to bring anything worse than PMS, then by all means I want to do what God tells me to do."

Eve was deceived by a talking snake, and then she became a talking snake. Apparently, Adam naively thought, "If Eve thinks it's a good idea, it must be." Adam listened to his wife instead of to God. Not only did Adam listen and eat, but there is no recorded word that he even questioned Eve or showed one hint of concern that she had not been obedient to God. He could have said, "Well, now you've done it. Didn't you listen to God? Where were you when He told us not to eat of this particular tree? Gracious Eve. If you act like this over a piece of fruit, what ever will you do when fast food chains come to our garden?"

The Word says in Genesis 3:6, "When the woman saw that the fruit of the tree was good for food and pleasing to the eye, and also desirable for gaining wisdom, she took some and ate it. She also gave some to her husband who was with her, and he ate it."

At that very moment, sin entered the human race and the whole world. Everything took a downward spiral from that point on. The flowers looked at each other and cried, "Help us. We need more water to drink or we will die. Get those nagging bugs off of us. Where did they come from anyway?"

The trees moaned to one another, "Help! What has happened to our limbs? They are drying up and rotting. If somebody doesn't do something quickly, we will be gone for sure.

The animals looked at each other and screamed. "Help! Our babies are sick, and our food is wasting away. Somebody help us."

Adam's toe got infected after he kicked the cursed tree, and Eve doubled over in pain from having a baby. Eve and Adam were the first to start on a walk to hell, and since that time, men and women have thought they had to follow. Had to follow? Wanted to follow? Felt compelled to follow? Needed to follow?

No matter the reason for the journey, Satan has carved out many roads, all leading us away from the smooth road called obedience to God and leading to the unbelievably tempting, cracked, muddy and icy road called disobedience. No one ever gets where they are going on the road called disobedience. Usually they get stuck in a ditch in which they feel there is no way out. The only way to get out of that ditch is to find the cross on which Jesus died, grab hold with all your might, and climb out to freedom.

What does this have to do with you and God's love for you? A lot. The whole Bible is the story of what God has been doing to make sure you knew He did not leave you helpless after the fall of Adam and Eve. He wanted to make sure that, fruit or no fruit, bite or no bite, He loved you. If you look closely in God's Word, you will find His kisses after the periods, in the margins and all over the quotation marks. If you'll put on your 3D glasses, you'll be shocked to find that God doodles. Hearts, drawn by His hand, line the margins and are filled with love messages straight to you. Your name is on each one. Some say, "I love you." Others beckon, "Be mine." Others invite, "I forgive you. Let's have a party."

When Eve and Adam disobeyed, they passed that disobedience trait down not only to you, but to everybody you know. That means that those who have dealt harshly with you, hurt you, scorned you, used you or treated you as if you had no sense, are all daily influenced by that same tree. That same fruit calls out to them as it calls you. "Try me. Take a bite. It will do something great for you. You'll feel better."

Speaking of feeling better, maybe what made someone else feel better when he hurt you has made you feel dirty, cheap and less than that for which you were created. Satan loves to hold that fruit in front of all men and women, enticing them to take the bait and therefore enjoy life at another's expense. If you have been bruised by the actions of any man or men, and your dreams have been painfully dropped in a deep well with the label "No Hope," God wants you to know that there is hope. You don't have to stay where you've been. You don't have to stay the way you are. You do not have to be somebody's victim, sexually, physically, or emotionally.

God has more for you. So much more. God wants you to know that He has a makeover plan for you. He wants to *make you over*, so that you may be new, and He wants to *make over you*, just because He loves you. He has been planning a large effort to drop some new joy right into your lap. It doesn't matter how old you are or how ingrained your patterns. You might have to make a decision in order to receive that joy, though. You might have to decide that you're worth it.

Maybe there exists in your mind a fertile field of cobwebs. Spiders play in that field, running in and out, spinning more webs, clogging your head with negatives, stinging you from time to time, and in general, creating quite a mess. You've tried to sweep out the problems, clean out the sticky webs, but somehow you've just not been successful. That's because you were never meant to clear out cobwebs by yourself. God wants to help you. Read the following love story from God's Word. The name may not be your name, but the situation might. It is from the Bible, from the book of Hosea.

Hosea married a prostitute named Gomer. Over and over, Gomer was drawn back to her past. Over and over, Hosea went to the more seedy side of town and looked for her. Again and again he found her, and each time he put his arms around her as he carried her home and said, "I love you."

We are Gomer. In an even greater way than Hosea loved Gomer, God loves us. God wants you to know that this is the way He feels about you. Whatever you're involved in, God is lovingly waiting for you, longing to wrap His arms around you and bring you back home to Him. This is the way God loves you. He loves you with energy and excitement, and He is thrilled because you are His daughter. He is busy every day trying to help you get that message. You are worth being a garden for love and not a garden for the spiders to nest. They will remain as long as you continue listening to the lies of Satan. They will remain as long as you allow Satan to call you Gomer.

We prostitute ourselves in several ways. Perhaps you know that you've used your body in ways that desecrate the high purposes God intended for you. It could be that a man forced you into initial encounters with sex and later you willfully chose to live a hidden lifestyle initiated by your first victimization. Or maybe no one forced you into anything, but because of pain with one relationship, you decided something else, even forbidden, might be better. One day, when you let down your guard, Satan slipped up behind you and showed you an enticing piece of fruit that seemed like the answer to all of your problems. He just didn't bother to tell you the rest of the story. He left off the part about how you would eventually feel because of your choice. He didn't tell you about your pain over this decision or about the pain you might cause someone else. But now tell me. If you were Satan, would you tell that?

Or maybe you have prostituted your mind. At first, you didn't even realize what was happening when the man or men in your life made sarcastic remarks to you about your intelligence. Maybe you didn't seem as bright as some. Or maybe you seemed brighter than others. Whatever, he didn't like it. You were either an embarrassment or a threat. You decided to act like you didn't measure up (when you really measured higher than he did in intelligence) or to just keep quiet rather than have harsh words make you feel stupid. Either way, you became a silent peacemaker, except you didn't get peace and nothing was ever silent. Your heartbeat of pain could be heard all through your body. Your anguish over what you couldn't talk about filtered into your dreams and caused a large rumbling in your chest.

You could have prostituted your emotions. Maybe you put them out on the playing field for anyone to grab, jump on, hurt, or throw away. Somewhere you got the idea that how you felt really didn't matter, and so you've spent years swallowing back toxic tears of pain, filling your insides with buckets of poison. After taking this abuse for many years, you woke up one morning to a new disease. Later, there was another one. Then, another. But, you hardly had time to notice. You were so busy fulfilling the role you had learned, that of working a little harder to get things done right, to avoid the criticism. But, you couldn't seem to ever get anything right. That same person always showed up, giving verbal and nonverbal reminders that you needed to work just a little bit harder.

Maybe you prostituted your heart. Someone made you feel like you did not measure up, and so you placed your heart in that man's path over and over again, standing like a child on tip toes, waiting for a panel of judges to declare you the winner. All you got was his judgment.

So, you set out to change his mind. You tried so hard. You did all the right things. You prepared the meals you knew he would like to eat. You kept the house spotlessly clean. You did everything you could to make him notice you. He never did. He never approved. He never recognized your worth.

What is your Father God doing during these times? He is standing in the background, right behind the pitcher who is doing his best to strike you out. God watches as you swing your bat, furiously trying to ward off another attack. When the game of life gets loud, boisterous and sometimes even dangerous, God runs up and down the field, cheering for you as you reach each base.

"That a girl! Keep going. That's my baby! Don't give up. Keep going. You'll make it. I'm right here behind you."

And, then, just as you stop running and take a breath, you look up. There are balloons floating all over the playing field, and they have your name on them. One says, "You're beautiful." Another says, "I'm so proud of you." And yet another, "I love you with my whole heart." Each is signed, "Your Father." You blush. Just then, you hear a plane and it's pulling a sign. You almost don't want to look. It has your name on it too. Does everybody see this?

"My arms of love are waiting for you," your Father.

Just as you start to run off the field from embarrassment, you suddenly notice that no one else sees the balloons or the plane. Whew. No one sees any of the signs. No one even sees your Father God running all over the field. The messages, you realize, are personal from your Father to you. You breathe a sign of relief, grateful to miss the sarcasm of the team, especially the pitcher.

Even though others may have hurt you, your real enemy is Satan. He is the one who is out to rob you of joy and destroy you. He uses people, but they aren't the real enemy. He is. Once you realize that, you will begin to see those who have victimized you as victims themselves.

We must guard against doing what Eve did when she allowed the enemy to influence her decision. Wherever you are sitting as you read this, put your book down for a minute and move toward a window. Look outside. The earth may be sunny, colorful and bright or frozen under winter ice. No matter. God is out there. He's out there, but He wants to come inside, where you are. He wants you to invite Him in to sit by you as you read. He wants to hold you through any pain you might be having. He wants to tell you that you matter a great deal to Him.

Will you join your Father on the dance floor and let His arms of love securely hold you? In your mind, become a child again, an eager girl not embarrassed to dance with your Father at the Father-Daughter Dance. Forget about impressing anybody with your dance skills. You don't need to have any. Whatever heavy load you have been carrying, you only need to fall into your Father's strong arms and allow Him to hold you and guide you through the dance. Oh, one more thing. He wants to give you something. Did you notice something in His hand? It will make the dance complete. It smells wonderful and looks elegant. It's pink and red and the colors are more vibrant than any you have ever seen.

Before you walk to the dance floor with your heavenly escort, won't you let him pin this beautiful corsage on your shoulder? After all, every lady deserves a corsage when she goes to a dance. Take in its fragrant smell. Enjoy. It's His gift to you.

Let His arms of love securely hold you. While you dance with Him, you will begin to feel your cares melting away, like winter snow when touched by the warmth of a new spring day.

To My Reader: Have you been living beneath the glorious privileges God has for you as His child? Has life worn you down in such a way that you cannot even see the love He wants to give you? Would you be surprised that He would run beside you when life gets tough just because you are His child? He cares deeply about whatever you are facing today. He cares so much that He wants to give good gifts to you. Will you receive what He has for you? It might be a smile from a child or a letter from a friend? He is trying to love you into knowing Him. We cannot limit the measures He will go to in order to achieve His goal. May I pray with you?

Prayer: Father, I am not used to thinking about you in these terms. I am not sure I can see you putting balloons in the air just to tell me you love me. But, I want my relationship with you to be just that personal, just that intimate. Will you help me? I'll step out to the Dance Floor, if you will be there to take my hand. In your Son's Name, Amen.

Chapter Four

The Rocking Chair Dance

Your Father God wants you, His daughter, to climb up in His lap and know the comfort and safety of being close to Him. You can trust His lap. It's safe there. His hands will only embrace you with genuine love. You can never be too old for His lap of love.

Maybe you're uncomfortable with this image. It could be that "close" is a scary thought for you. You always hold your guard and want to be in control. You move toward others, men as well as women acquaintances, with a hesitant step. You keep a clear list of "do not!" memorized in your head.

Do not let them into your world. *Do not* become emotionally involved. *Do not* have physical contact. *Do not* allow hugs.

When you're alone in the quietness of your home, you are finally able to let go and relax, though a gnawing restlessness continues to stir deep memories of hidden pain. Some days, you are okay. Other days you silently cry, get angry and shake your fist at God, asking, "Why? Where were you when these things happened to me?"

One thing I am learning about our loving God is that He is under no obligation to answer my questions. When He made covenant with me, He didn't whisper, "B.J., just give me your list. I'll answer each of them right away. Maybe even today."

That's how we want Him to work, but as always, He has His own agenda. Most of us, at one time or another, ask, "Where *were* you, God?" Or maybe, in your present pain and heartbreak, you are crying, "Where *are* you?"

God has arranged this world and its people so that He is dependent on us to do His work. He is in control and in charge of the workings of the universe, but we are co-workers with Him. We are in a co-responsibility with Him in His mission to redeem all of creation.

As you have grown older and evaluated your younger days, perhaps you are now dealing with the first realizations that your memories of a certain man in your life were not pleasant ones. You may be grown and yet still dealing with bad memories of your father, or painful memories of your brother, or scary memories of your uncle. It may be that you are dealing with a continual stream of poor decisions through your dating or marriage choices, leading you to conclude that, for whatever reasons, happiness just wasn't in the picture for you. On some days, your self-image is so tarnished that you want to sink behind the crowd of people so others won't notice you.

Wait. Do you hear it? It's that familiar and soothing rhythm of a chair going back and forth. There's that creak that happens every time the forward motion begins again. Steady. Continual. Rock. Back and forth rock. Rock you can count on. Rock you can depend on. Back and forth. Comforting rock. Can you hear the rocking chair of God?

When my son, Shawn, was tiny and could barely talk or walk, he came up to me, held his arms up and said, "Mama, rock me." My response was always the same. "With pleasure." After hearing this many times, Shawn walked up to me one day, held up his hands and said, "Mama, rock me with pleasure."

It was always a pleasure to rock my two sons. It is God's pleasure to rock you, no matter how old you may be right now. God doesn't see you as fifteen or fifty, forty or ninety. He sees you as His daughter, and He loves you. He cherishes those moments when you hold up your arms and say, "Father, rock me." He treasures the pleasure of your company.

Take a second now and look at God's lap. It's empty. He saved it today just for you. He wants you to climb up, lay your head on His shoulder, and draw comfort from the steady back and forth rock of His chair. Like the rhythm of His dance, the rocking chair's movement enfolds you, covers you, and embraces you so that you are swept up into the comforting steady rock. Back and forth the chair goes. Just like your faithful Father God, the chair that goes back will surely come forward. When it goes forward, it will surely go back. Like God. Back and forth. Steady. Dependable.

God does not stop in the middle of the rock and decide to leave the chair in a backward position for months or years. He doesn't quit the soothing constant sound so that He can stop in the forward position and stay there. He never just stays there. He is always moving in a direction you need. When the chair goes back, He whispers, "I love you." When the chair goes forward, He whispers, "I love you."

Your Father God won't play tricks on you as He rocks you. He won't rock the chair backwards, take another look at you and then decide you're not worth staying along for the complete ride. He won't move the chair forward, look down the street, find someone else He'd rather have, and decide to drop you off before He makes the chair rock back again. Your Father God will not compare you with any other daughter. While you are in His lap of love, you won't hear one word about another's prettier face or skin, another's better figure or smarter wardrobe. You won't hear Him say, "I wish you looked like her."

He will be constantly, consistently devoted to you and to the love relationship He desires for the two of you. While you are in His lap, you will never hear Him singing His song to anyone else.

In His lap of security, He will never tell you that you're not good enough, or that you just don't measure up, or that you never seem to get things done. He'll never say that you are lazy, or fat, or that your face is too full of pimples. Instead, He is full of surprises, and He plans exciting dances in your honor.

He values every flaw you have, and would even send engraved invitations to a *You're Pretty Party* in your honor. At this dance, your Father chooses to dance every dance with you, the one who never feels good about her appearance.

To the daughter who abhors her weight, thinking no one could possibly love her, he holds a *That Doesn't Matter To Me* Party, and makes you feel that you are the most desired girl there.

For the one who has always resented her short stature, feeling that if she were taller she would surely be noticed, He sends hand-written invitations for a *You're Tall Enough For Me Formal.* You appear, standing short in your prettiest dress, and He tells you that you're just the right size for this dance with Him.

My earthly Father didn't spoil me with riches. He never indulged my childish whims or fanciful dreams. He stood on the conservative side in my requests for pretty clothes and new gadgets. I didn't grow up expecting him to buy me anything. There was one area, however, in which he did spoil me, and that area seemed to make up for anything else that was lacking. He spoiled me thoroughly with his hugs, and usually they were preceded by a complement. My given name was Betty Jo. Being his baby, my daddy called me Baby Jo. I endured, (and sometimes loved) that name way into my adult life.

When I look back at pictures of me as a child and teenager, I can only be grateful that my father saw me as he did. Until high school, I was taller than most girls in my class. I had skinny bird legs, which were perched under an unbelievably skinny torso. That torso was attached to a very plain face that appeared small in comparison to my full head of long coarse hair. That hair was either in a pony tail or pig tails, and that face had no clue about makeup until my friends sat me down in my junior year of high school and showed me what color could do for white cheeks and pale lips.

For some reason, I didn't think of myself as unattractive. I didn't have jealous fits over my friends' dates. I didn't sit around dreaming about the day my ugly ducking appearance would turn into a swan.

That's because, in my father's eyes, I already was a swan. He saw me as his precious baby girl, and it never dawned on me that the rest of the world didn't view me that way, too. Some of my fondest memories are of the days I would dress for church and model for my father. Never mind that my coarse hair wasn't completely in place or that my long legs took up most of my body. Never mind that my long skinny arms reached almost down to my ankles. When I walked into the room, my father stood up, started whistling, and began acting crazy. Like a father in love with his daughter.

He would call, "Oh Mama, come quick. Get me my gun. All the boys are going to be after our baby today. Wooooo-eeeeee. She is something else!"

He loved being a clown anyway, but the thing is, I actually believed what he was saying. He ranted on and on about my appearance. His lines were familiar and repetitive. Sometimes, he'd call loudly, "Mama, Come quick. Let's go to the store. I've got to buy an electric fence to keep all the boys away from Baby Jo."

He whistled a boy's whistle at me, did a little two-step dance of joy, prancing around the living room and snapping his fingers in rhythm, acting like someone on drugs. But, I loved it. I even bought into it. (And I was old enough to know better. Mirrors were in our home!)

I guess the fact that hardly any of those boys ever came around didn't really bother me. For some reason, at that point in my life, my father's affirmation was larger than life. It was all I needed. I was happy with the way people treated me, and my life was extremely full and active. Even if the boys never came around, that was okay. My father thought they should have, and that was good enough for me. His affirmation convinced me that one day they would.

My earthly father now lives in heaven. I wouldn't be surprised if he doesn't, at this very hour, have a group of angels in five or six long lines, teaching them his two-step dance of joy, along with his little prance and the snapping of his rhythmic fingers. Maybe they will all be sent out as cheering squads for the many girls and women who never had a father to make over them. My father would like that.

No matter what negatives your earthly father said to you about your appearance, your Heavenly Father views your differently. He never considers you an ugly duckling on the way to becoming a swan. To Him, you already *are* a swan.

No matter how old you get, no matter how many wrinkles move upon your face to threaten your youth, no matter how heavy your weight, your Heavenly Father's lap is still available. You will never get too old for His embrace of love. You will never do anything bad enough that will keep Him from rocking you in His rocking chair. You can never stray too far away, thereby ruining your chances and making Him decide He'll give His lap to another.

His initial plan was that we would fellowship with Him. Fellowship implies communication. Communication involves talking and listening. Tragically, not too many of us are doing much of either as far as God is concerned. We have trained ourselves to do most of the talking when we pray. Few of us have experience in listening to what the Father might have to say to us.

Listen carefully. Turn off the television. Don't answer the phone. Try to quiet the other voices around you until you hear only your Father's voice. I know it's hard, but try. God wants you to hear the comforting sound of wood going back and forth. He wants you to hear the familiar squeak of an old chair that has been used a lot. He wants you to pull away from the hurts of this day as you listen to the sound of His big rocking chair.

Join your Father in the Rocking Chair Dance, the most soothing of all the dances. You don't have to do anything but relax in His lap. The chair does all the work.

As the chair goes back and forth, know that He is waiting. He'll even help you climb in. Hold up your arms. Ask your Father God to rock you.

His answer will always be the same. "With pleasure."

To My Reader: It may be difficult for you to think of yourself as a pleasure to God. You see yourself with critical eyes. Can you imagine, though, that God might take those things you consider faults and see them in an entirely different way? He made you. He loves you just as you are. I would like to encourage you to climb into His rocking chair, and allow yourself the luxury of doing simply nothing except letting your Father love you.

Prayer: Dear Father, I see myself in a realistic way. Actually, I see myself in a critical way. Some days, there doesn't seem to be much to like. I would love to begin to think of myself as a pleasure to you. Just the sound of that brings me into thoughts I have not allowed myself to think. Show me how to accept that I am your pleasure. In Jesus' Name, Amen.

Chapter Five

They're Playing Our Song

Whether intended or not, some women get a message of being in someone's way. They begin to feel they are a mistake!

It's hard to get out of bed each morning feeling you are a disappointment.

If you feel that you are a disappointment, then you are living under an impossible burden. Daily, you undermine your own abilities because you are so busy trying to figure out what you can do to please others.

You try to say and do the right things, but it never is good enough. Sometimes you just feel everyone would be better off if you weren't around. Whether spoken verbally or implied, you get the definite message that others would like nothing better than for you to literally get lost.

Women swallow these hurtful messages, allowing them to sit in our souls while we try to go on living.

Outwardly, we're smiling and acting like we couldn't be happier. Inwardly, we turn into buckets of pain each time another sends us that same demeaning message. It's as if we have an imaginary knife sitting on our heart, and that knife has the ability to magically make another notch every time the same hurt is given. We have so cleverly closed ourselves off from feeling pain that we aren't even aware how deeply we are cut.

If you are a woman in pain from this type of negative message, your Father God is especially tuned into you. His eyes of love weep over the injustices you have been handed. To you, and all women like you, He sends out a loving call to allow Him to be the Father, Husband, Brother that you need. He wants to redeem what has been taken from you. That means you will have to make a decision to allow Him to fill in those hurt places in your life with His Life. You will consciously choose to spend some time with Him, get to know Him, and purposefully let His kindness override the hurts.

There is one more thing. Stop and touch your heart right now. Remember? There is something sewn into the lining of that same heart. Your Heavenly Father put it there when He made you. It's your personal love invitation, the one He sewed with thread that would never wear out! Remember what He wrote?

Despite what any person might have said to you, or how he might have made you feel, your Heavenly Father has a different message. He tells you that you are His dream girl. As far as He's concerned, there is nothing about you that isn't just right. Instead of telling you to "Get lost!" He says to you, "Get found! Get found by your Heavenly Father! We have so much joy to share. Let me find you! Let me find you and hold you in a forever embrace of love!"

How very sad that someone could belch his poison into you, thus passing on to you a fragile self-concept. Daily. Slowly. Monthly. Year after year. Your whole self suffered because of it. Somewhere in between the years that used to be and the years that now are, you lost yourself. Your self-concept ran away and hid.

Your heavenly Father has no intention of leaving you in the garbage can of another's discontent! You have value that you've never recognized! You have abilities you've never noticed! There is so much more to you than what another's sickness or dysfunction has told you. There are trails of flower bulbs, resting beneath the surface of your life, begging to blossom and send perfumed fragrance into all of your pain. Your Heavenly Father has been trying to tell you this for so long! He's been sending His love messages day after day, but of course, you never heard Him. He understands this, too. He understands because He knows you were too busy trying to play the human game.

Here's how the human game goes. There are two players, you and the person on the other side. Your goal is to get that person to notice you. You're the underdog from the get-go. You have to work extra hard to win.

This is how the human game begins. The other side, which would be any hurtful influence in your life, always goes first. He not only goes first, but he always throws the dice, always moves first, and always has the first and last try. He is in a win-win situation. You, however, are the opponent. You never go first. You never throw the dice, and you never have a try. You are in a lose-lose situation.

That's the human game you learned to play, and you probably learned that game well.

There's another game that is completely different from the human game; it's the God game. Here's how it's played. Your heavenly Father is on one side and you are on the other. But wait. He's coming over to your side. Does that mean you need to go to the other side? But wait. When you do that, He goes over to the other side with you. You repeat this God game over and over, never ending up on opposite sides. Finally, you catch on.

In the God game, there are no opposite sides. God stands by your side, stays by your side, and remains by your side. Even if you should try to out run Him to the other side, you can't. He's faster than you are! So, He is always, always right by your side. That's where He wants to be.

All during those difficult years when you thought you didn't measure up to an earthly being's expectations, your heavenly Father tried to get His message to you. Daily, He called out to you these words: *You do matter. You do have worth.* Sadly, the human game blocked your hearing. You focused on that game, rather than on listening to God.

What you *are* is not determined by someone else's expectations. You are not a disappointment.

You are not a mistake. Those are seeds placed in your head by someone who was hurting and angry. Those seeds have been watered by that same person and fed by that same person for so many years that the seeds have sprouted. The sprouts aren't pretty. They look like weeds. They're heavy. They take up too much space. They carry a rancid odor.

The only way you can get rid of those weeds is to allow Gardener God to use His supernatural weed eater! If you choose to let Him begin, He *can* make a difference in your life! It's time for you to stop listening to the lies from Satan and begin listening to the truth from God! Satan loves to see you defeated, depressed, and with no hope! Remember, no matter what any one did to you, that person was not and is not the enemy. Satan is the Enemy, but he does a grand job of "passing the buck!" He likes to make us think that human beings are the enemy. That's not true. The enemy is Satan.

Maybe somewhere in your life, someone gave you the message that you were *not as good* as others. Soon you began to think of your name as *Not As Good*.

Your Heavenly Father wants to change your name from *Not As Good* to *You Belong To Me*. He has that right. He made you.

Your heavenly Father wants you to know that, no matter how awful anyone else has made you feel, that person was wrong. He might have been tired or overworked, but he was still wrong. The only way you can change a negative stamp of disapproval is to actively seek your heavenly Father's new name for you! You won't get it by whining or complaining. You won't get it through self- pity. Your new name comes only as you invite that name to be yours.

So, if this description is you, begin singing this new song today. The name of the song is *You Belong To Me,* a grand description of the way God made you to be, a creation of great worth! It's been number one on the charts for months now. I'm surprised you've never heard it because it was written just for you! It's your song of love! The songwriter is God. The musician is God.

For you, just as for any other women who have felt they never measured up, this song brings victory. No longer do you have to live under the negative messages someone else inflicted. Live, instead, at the finish line. Reach the goal of decision. Decide to let go of those messages you never deserved. Decide to receive the new message that you are worthy, you are special, and you've never been a mistake.

Shhhh. Listen. It's the angels. They're playing music just for you! They're singing *You Belong To Me!* Now watch. Your Heavenly Father reaches His hands out to you. He turns His head toward the angels and begins humming *You Belong To Me* along with them. Go ahead. Walk to the dance floor.

Receive the wonderful news. Listen to your heavenly Father as He whispers in your ear. "My darling child. You are accepted by me. Rest right here in my arms. Let's dance once more. Can you hear it? They're playing our song."

To My Reader: Have you struggled with trying to please someone and trying to measure up to their expectations? Have you faced sarcasm and ridicule from those who felt it was their life's purpose to make you feel low and unnecessary? Your Father does not want you to suffer under that sort of condemnation any longer. He wants you to know that you belong to Him, and in that realization, you will always measure up. Believe it.

Prayer: I like the sound of my voice when I call you Father. I'm getting more and more comfortable with the knowledge that I matter to you. I want to know you better and better. I want to accept your love and I want to learn to love you back. In your Son's Name, Amen.

Chapter Six

A Wallflower No More
(The Dance of Faith)

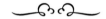

Have you ever been a wallflower? It doesn't feel so good. You sit on the sidelines, watching everyone else dance, but never getting to dance yourself. You don't have a partner. So, you watch and wait, hoping someone will invite you to dance. There's nothing you can do to lure attention to your corner. You try smiling or looking as pretty as a picture, but nothing can make that guy come your way. You get up and go to the water fountain, thinking maybe someone will notice you as you pass by, but no one does. Sitting on the sidelines, never being included, is a desperate feeling. With no chances to dance, you miss all the fun. With no chances to dance, you give yourself a message: *Something must be wrong with me, or someone would ask me to dance. Something must be wrong with me, or somebody would want to be with me.*

You question things about yourself. Is it the way I look? Am I no fun? Am I not a good dancer?

So, you sit at a table by yourself. The lights are low and the room is beautiful. There is chatter all around you. Laughter comes from some of the dancers, but you're not a part of the fun. You wait, biting your nails and trying to act like you didn't come to the dance to dance anyway! You like sitting by yourself. Alone. In a corner. No excuse makes you feel better. You're a wallflower! Watching from a distance, you feel you are not important enough to be included in the dance.

But that was a dance. What about life? Have you felt like a wallflower in your home? In your work? Do you look from a distance at relationships that were made to be enjoyed, but instead are only endured? You look from a distance at your dreams. You sit on the side of the dance floor, never knowing the joy of getting up and moving forward.

What's keeping you from the dance? Who blocks your chance to sway with the music of the life God has planned for you? You may be fifteen or seventy, but the feelings inside are the same. Rejection doesn't choose age or capability. Rejection doesn't discriminate between the rich and the not-so-rich. Rejection even sends its hateful fangs into the pretty as well as the not so pretty. Who has told you that you aren't worthy of the dance?

When your Father God created you, He made you to be in a relationship with Him and with others. You were created to interact, to receive communication, to tell your side of things. You weren't created simply to close up and be quiet. He made you to enter into the dance.

Through the years, however, you gradually moved to the sidelines of life. You became a wall-flower. How did it happen? When did it happen? Is there any hope that you can move away from the sidelines and seek Life?

You can. You can find God's arm and enter into the dance with Him. It's a private dance, after all, between the two of you. It involves an intimate exchange of love, trust, and friendship. This dance will divert your attention from the pain in your life. With your Father God, you no longer have to be a wallflower.

Have you ever thought about the second part of that compound word, wallflower? It's *flower*. It seems like an oxymoron, for how can you sit under layers of wall and yet be a flower? What an abso-lutely beautiful picture of the mercy your Father God wants to give you today! Attached to the negative is a positive! Attached to what you think you are is a refreshing reminder of who you are supposed to be! This is God's way. Into the dough of negative, God always throws in a batch of positive.

Your Father God wants you to know that you are a flower. You are His flower, and He longs to walk into your garden to dwell with you. He longs to hold you in His embrace of love. It was never His inten-tion that you become a wall of pain. He hurts for you. He wants a better life for you. He knows how to lay before you the desires of your heart! He knows how to help you find those desires.

To your Father God, you are a center-stage flower! You deserve the best! You deserve the applause of the crowd as you shyly begin to move onto the dance floor. No one will clap louder than He will. No one will view you with eyes of love more that Him.

This might all sound like too much to comprehend. For you, how can life ever be different? Would walking onto the dance floor, choosing life and allowing God to embrace you really make a difference? *Yes!* Still, you are likely thinking, "Well, that may work for some; but no one really knows my situation. It won't work for me." That's where faith comes in.

There is a wonderful story of faith in the book of Luke (8:43-48). This story is about a woman who had turned into a wallflower, and then later became a bright new flower because of Jesus. She had a physical problem that caused her to keep to herself, watching others join the dance while she remained on the sidelines. Who wanted her anyway? She could not stop bleeding. So bad was her malady that Jewish men were not allowed to even look at her! Their Jewish law stated that to even touch a woman like this would make a man unclean. Imagine the loneliness she endured! This went on for twelve long years.

Forced to be a wallflower, this woman likely walked with her head down so that she would not make eye contact with a man. Should she decide to go out of her home, she possibly would have gone during the dark hours of night to protect men who might be on the streets during daylight. She was probably laughed at and made to keep her distance.

Some might have even called her a freak.

Surely, she was weak after a twelve-year loss of blood. Her life had been reduced to two realities, loneliness and sickness, and she carried both with a painful weight. Nobody wanted her around. The men scorned her and the women shunned her. They didn't try to understand what she was going through.

Whatever money she had was now gone. She had spent it all on doctors who could never find a cure. Years ago, when the bleeding first began, perhaps the neighborhood ladies decided that this woman either had an evil spirit or she was being punished by God for some sin in her life. No one listened as she tried to explain that she could not help her situation. Eventually, she stopped trying and resorted to living the best she could as a loner.

On a particularly beautiful day, this woman heard that Jesus, the Healer, was passing by. A healer passing by? A healer coming her way? She had to find out about Him. She had to take a chance. Other stories had drifted into her town about this Healer named Jesus. The stories were electrifying and confusing at the same time. The word on the street was that this Jesus could actually heal people just by touching them. Faith that had long ago died began to stir within this sick woman; then reality hit and she knew there was no way to even see Jesus. She couldn't go among the crowds. Her outcast condition mandated a secluded life, in spite of the hope Jesus offered.

She could not stop thinking about the unbeliev-able difference her life could have if she could just get to the Healer. Could it be? Could it possibly be that she, even she, could be healed? She had to find out. It was worth a try. A try? It was worth every-thing. What did she have to lose? She had been a wallflower for too long now. It was time to step out in faith and find the Dance.

On that day when Jesus passed by in the street, a huge crowd gathered around Him. She thought she had no chance, with so many clamoring for His atten-tion. Those who gathered were curious about Him, wondering about Him, eager to learn more, but only one in the crowd had faith enough to make her way through the huge crowd crushing around Him. The Bible doesn't give us all the details, but imagine with me this scenario.

Some men recognized her and quickly moved away. Others pushed her back. "This is not for YOU," they yelled in her face. "This man wants nothing to do with a woman who is sick! He has better things to do today." Others jeered, "Remember your place. You are a wallflower. Stay on the outside. We don't want you here."

She made a decision to approach the Healer from his back so He wouldn't have to look at her either. It would be better if she crawled through the crowd, hiding her identity. Several times she fell beneath the huge movement of men trying to get close to Jesus. One man's scornful look sent cold chills all into her. "Get away from here," he screamed. "We all know who you are. You are not the kind of person Jesus wants around. You're not who we want around, either. Go back to your home."

Some in the crowd laughed. Others joined in the jeering. Each time someone recognized her, she was pushed further back. These men had no idea that her determination was now at the point of no return. She *would* get through, no matter what they said or did to her. This was her last chance in life. There was no more fight left.

"Rabbi," many were calling, "Come over this way."

"Rabbi," others said, "Tell us about your kingdom."

"Rabbi," still others added, "Stay in our town for the night."

Softly, so that no one heard her, she remembered the hope that had begun in her when she first learned of Jesus. "Rabbi," she whispered to herself, "if I can just touch the edge of your clothes, I can get what I need."

Down low, crawling slowly, she was not noticed as much. She heard His voice and realized she was getting close to Him. Dare she stand? No, she couldn't chance it. Someone would recognize her.

Having grown accustomed to being overlooked, she had no right to stand anyway. Her place in life had been long established. Others had taught her who she was. Her name was Neglected. Her name was Nuisance. Her name was Never-Mind-Her. She knew her place.

Today, however, her name was Faith, and as that determination moved within her, she knew she had to keep trying. Suddenly, someone from behind moved closer with a question, and when Jesus stopped to answer, she moved closer too. She could hear His voice now, a voice unlike the harsh voices of the men who scorned her in the city streets. There was something compelling, commanding and yet gentle about His voice. A calming wave swept through her. She was not afraid anymore. Within His voice, she found the hope she sought. Because of His voice, she found her own voice. Courage sprang up, and before she considered any man's disapproval, she was inches away from Him. Her hand moved forward, as she once again whispered to herself, "If I can just touch the edge of His clothing, I can get everything I need. If I can just touch this Healer, I can be rid of my sickness. I don't need for Him to give me His time or attention. I just need a touch. I'll do this quietly and then leave."

Jesus began walking about the same time she touched his clothing. Instantly, she felt a surge of power going through her body. Sheets of electrical current moved in such a way that she couldn't move if she wanted to. Strong, yet gentle. Forceful, yet comfortable. So this is how healing feels? She could tell within her body that the blood was drying up. The cramping stopped, the backache ceased as energy drained became energy restored. She began to cry with thanksgiving as she turned to slowly crawl back to her place on the outside of society.

Suddenly, something happened that she had not counted on at all. Jesus stopped and said, "Who touched me? I just felt power leaving me. Who touched me?"

Some of the men around Jesus said, "How would we know? There are so many people around you that most of us are bumping against each other. We don't know who touched you."

When Jesus continued to question, the woman felt she had to confess. She turned back around and fell at His feet. Would He condemn her for her actions? Would He make her feel she was not worthy of freedom? Would He tell the others to cast her away from this group?

In the recognition of her healing came new hope. She would take her chances with His reaction as well as the reaction of all those around Jesus. When she opened her mouth to speak, she felt strong and capable. She had received what she wanted, and all doubt about her place in society was taking a back seat in her mind. She was important. She did matter. Her life would never be the same.

"I did it," she said as she looked up at his face.

Jesus said this one wonderful word that changed her world forever. He called her Daughter. Daughter!! He brought her into His family and made her His child. Daughter! Nothing had ever sounded so good to her in all her life.

"Daughter, your faith has made you whole."

Those words began jumping around inside of her. *Daughter, faith, made whole*. It had been so long since she had smiled. Now, she couldn't stop.

"Go in peace," he smiled back at her.

He moved on. Someone else needed Him. The crowd moved with Him, and she was left on the ground in that Holy spot where He had stood. Some looked at her strangely as they passed. Others ignored her. Still, a few gave her the look she had always gotten from them, a look that said, "Get away from us. You don't belong here."

No matter. She knew better. She did belong here. She belonged. As she stood to walk home, her new energy engaged her steps, but her thoughts were on the words He had said to her. She would tuck them into her heart and keep them there forever. If anyone ever questioned her place again, she would know better. No one could take this away from her.

She walked away a new woman. From bent down and fearful to standing straight and smiling. The words echoed through her body. "Daughter, Faith, Healed, Peace. Daughter, Faith, Healed, Peace." They were her words. She would never be the same again.

What about you? Have you been made to feel you belong on the sidelines of life? Has anyone made you feel you don't even deserve to look him in the eye? Well, today is your day to come out of hiding. Just as this woman in the story moved forth, so must you. Claiming the dance is an act of your will. You have to take the first step away from the wall. You have to choose faith in order to move away from the corner. Starting right now, you can decide that you are worth far more than you've thought you are. You are a precious prize to your Heavenly Father, and to make the move from being a victim, you will need to view yourself as a prize.

Maybe you're thinking, "I am anything *but* a prize!" When your Father formed you, He thought you were a prize, a jewel, a thing to treasure. He still feels that way. Every time you allow yourselves to be put down by another, made to feel less than the prize that you are, another layer of wall is added to your body. You become a real wallflower, with layer after layer after layer of walls. No wonder you don't even know who you are anymore. No wonder you've forgotten what it's like to feel needed, wanted or loved.

It has nothing to do with how you feel today or how you will feel tomorrow. It has nothing to do with outer circumstances. Claiming the dance is an inner reality, a decision whose main focus is with one primary relationship. That relationship, the one with your Father God, is a relationship that can make a difference in how you handle all other relationships. Your circumstances might not change, but there is a way to allow Him to make a difference. There is a way to pull aside from the hurts and find nourishment, encouragement and love from your Creator. He can make all the difference in your life! Your inner soul will begin to feed on this difference.

Knowing that God loves you as His daughter will cause you to look for Him every day. You will want to get up in the morning and speak to Him right away. You will desire to try to know Him better through talking and walking with Him. You will want to know more about Him. He already knows all there is to know about you.

What He wants to tell you today is this. "Join me in Life's Dance. Move forward. Walk toward Me. Believe in Me. Step out to be healed. Pay no attention to those negative voices around you. This is our dance. Not theirs. Even if you try to explain it, they won't understand.

"Take a chance. You are my Daughter. Safe in my arms, you will be a wallflower no more."

To My Reader: Have you been standing on the sidelines of life, wanting to participate but feeling you are not welcomed? Are you ready to walk toward your Heavenly Father, take His hand, and join Him in this dance of Faith? Whatever has been making you feel neglected and hopeless can be changed by just a touch of His robe. If you need a prayer, I'd like to offer one.

Prayer: Dear God, you know better than anyone how lonely I am. You know that I often feel left out and unworthy. I am like this woman, in that I have allowed the unkind ways of others to dig my ditch of pain a little deeper. I don't want to do that anymore. I need your strong hand to remind me that I really do matter, that I really do have purpose. Give me the gift of faith that I may begin to reach out and claim a new life with you. In Jesus' Name, Amen.

Chapter Seven

The Step-On-Your-Toes Dance

Do you remember the very first time you got on the dance floor to sway to the music of a romantic tune? You were probably in the seventh or eighth grade. Your palms were sweaty, your hands were trembling, and your feet? Well, you had no idea what to do with them. They seemed huge to you as you fumbled along, counting to yourself, one and step slide, two and step slide, three and step slide, four and step slide. Were you supposed to put your right foot out first or your left? What if you ended up ready to step and slide your right foot when it was actually time to step and slide your left foot? Oh, the humiliation of those first awkward dances. The embarrassment. The torment.

Your partner was probably just as hesitant as you. He had to guide you, hold your hand, but not too tightly, think of something interesting to ask you, and still do those crazy step slide counts! More than once, he probably said, "Oh dear! I'm sorry!" as he awkwardly stepped on your toes. By the end of the night, you were ready to run home, take off your shoes, and place your two left feet into a tub off warm water! Ouch! Eeek! Help! Did your young partner have no mercy at all? You vowed it would be a freezing night in June before you ever put yourself through that again!

While stepping on your toes wasn't planned or intended, it happened anyway. Why? Because there wasn't enough room in the tiny space between your bodies for four feet to be in charge. Two feet had a hard enough time as it was. The perfect formula for this dance was two feet leading and two feet following. When four feet tried to lead, or when four feet tried to follow, toes got in the way. Feet that were designed to lead found that alone they could handle the dance floor just fine! Feet designed to follow found that easy, too, as long as another pair of feet weren't in the way. Together, however, those four feet on the dance floor became a source for pain. A negative formula. A "don't want to ever do *this* again" event.

When your Father God invites you for this particular dance, He's aware that you're a bit timid. This is new territory, after all. A risk. A "can't we just skip this?" challenge. Before He moves to the floor with you, He invites you to sit down in a chair by Him while the two of you talk. He tells you that this will be new for you, and He understands how hard it will be to follow His lead. He tells you that sometimes you will move your feet the wrong way, placing your foot in the path of His foot, and then your toes will get stepped on. He tells you not to run to your seat the first time this happens. He asks you not to rebel against Him when this happens. If you will stay on the dance floor with Him, allowing Him to lead while you follow, the rhythm of life will flow in a comforting, refreshing pattern. You will learn from Him. After this Father-Daughter talk, you both slowly move to the dance floor.

You stand close to your Father, a feeling of complete security falling all over you. He holds up His left hand, palm out, inviting you to rest your right hand in His. You do, and the feeling of your small hand in His large hand completely overcomes you. You start to tremble, but your Father's hand steadies you, as He takes His right arm and lovingly pulls you close to His heart. The dance begins. You wonder if anything could ever be any better than this! What strength He has! What perfect balance you feel next to Him! What complete freedom is yours! You remember the song from the *King and I*, and begin to think you really could dance all night.

You start to glide on the dance floor, completely immersed in total joy! A vision forms in your mind. You imagine your girlfriends from junior high days, the ones who thought you never quite measured up. "If they could only see me now," you imagine. "They would look at me and envy this dance! Never again would I be the subject of their ridicule! In one quick moment, I would gain the recognition I've always wanted!"

OUCH! "Father," you stumble. "That hurt! You just stepped on my toes!"

"I had the feeling I had lost your attention. Had you taken your eyes off Me, by some chance?"

"Well, maybe a little," you confess, "but it surely would be nice if my friends could see me now!"

"Would it really?" your Father questions. "Your motives would be wrong. We would have to start this dance over again."

"Over again? Why?"

"Because you didn't learn the first step of the dance."

"The first step? What is that?"

"The first step is submission. You, My daughter, can't submit to My leadership as long as you're using Me for selfish reasons. You want all the girls to envy your position with Me on the dance floor. I want you out here for one reason only. I want you to love My dance."

"I'll try." The dance resumes.

All over the dance floor He carries you, with breath-taking movements of life. This is complete joy, a combination of total freedom and happiness! You gaze around the floor. On one side in a quiet corner where no one is noticing, a couple you know well is enjoying their own dance. Have they noticed you yet? You're not quite sure. They have to! They just have to!

OUCH! "Father, that hurts! You stepped on my toes again!"

"I was wondering why you were pulling Me over to the corner, moving your feet away from My leading? It doesn't work that way. Not only are you pulling against Me, but also you're trying to brag on our relationship! No, it doesn't work that way at all. You're trying to be seen with Me, for others to notice our relationship. I want you on the dance floor for only one reason. I want you to love My dance."

Your Father holds you close once again, and you realize that nothing you could ever want could be better than this. The beauty of His presence is overwhelming. For a minute, you shut your eyes, allowing Him to lead as you follow.

Suddenly, you hear a muffled sound behind you. Quickly, you turn to see a crowd gathered, all eyes gazing at the center of the crowd. What's that all about? Surely, your Father wants to check this out, too. Someone could be hurt. Somebody could need you.

OUCH! "Father, that really hurts! You stepped on my toes again!"

"What was so interesting behind you that you would neglect the One in front of you?"

"I don't know, Father. I just assumed You'd want to see what was happening, too! Don't You want to know what's going on back there? Aren't You compelled to make sure You're not needed?"

"Not as long as I'm needed right here. Not as long as I'm guiding you. Besides, how can you assume what I'm thinking? How can you assume where I want to go on the dance floor? Can you assume My will? You want to be on the dance floor to take Me places *you* want to go. I only want you to love My dance."

Once again, your Father started the dance. It was wonderful. Refreshing. Beautiful. Then why were you crying? An overwhelming sense of shame makes your face turn hot, as a stream of tears begins to fall. How dare you think you could dance with God? What makes you think you're worthy of this high honor? He knows about your past! He knows everything!

OUCH! "Why did You step on my toes, Father? I'm not going in a direction different from You this time! I'm right here with You."

"You think that because you are on the floor with Me that you are really *with Me?*

You're living your past again, blaming yourself for those sins we've already discussed, those mistakes I've already forgiven. Why would you come to the dance floor with Me and look back? I know the plans I have for you. Plans to prosper you. Plans to give you hope and a future. (Jeremiah 29:11) Those plans do not include eating from the table of old sins. Let them go! Enjoy My dance. I'm inviting you to love My dance."

It seems you remain on the floor for a long time before the clattering of dishes, the clanging of glasses, and the chatter of people grows loud in your ears. Meanwhile, your Father hums a soothing song of grace as He continues moving you in the dance of life. The noises of others become louder, calling for your attention. Finally, you speak; at the exact time your toes begin to hurt once again."

"Ouch! What did I do now? You just don't understand! I've got to go see what that noise is all about! It's wonderful out here on life's floor with you, Father, but after all, I do have a job. I do have friends who need me. I have to put the dishes in the dishwasher and start a load of clothes. My car needs to be in the repair shop, my bills need to be mailed, and I need to shop! I'm almost out of makeup and hair spray. Will You wait for me? I won't be long."

Patiently, your Father agrees to wait, but first He offers a suggestion. "Can I go with you? We can still be close while you run your errands. We can still move in the same rhythm of life while you shop."

"Well, I don't know, Father. I don't think You'd enjoy shopping with me very much. How would I explain Your Presence to others? I've got calls to return on my cell phone and e-mails to send. Can't You just wait for me? I'll be back. When I get back, we'll do the church thing. I'll get real still and listen to everything You want to say to me. I promise. Right now, I really need to go."

You show up, hours later, looking for God. He's right where you left Him. Waiting. Running to His side, you exclaim, "See, I told you I'd be back. I finished. Here I am, all yours. Let's dance again!"

Your Father can't help but notice the new outfit and shining black heels, and with every move, your Father steps on your toes.

"Ouch! Ouch! Father, what's that all about? Why can't I even dance any more without Your stepping on my toes? With every move You step on my toes. What's going on?"

"I work best when I'm not someone's convenience. It's all or nothing. My dance is a never-ending waltz. You came back to Me dressed for church! I really don't care what you wear to church! What I care about is that you love My dance."

As the dance continues, you ask your first real question. Then another and another. Your voice sounds tired.

"Why is this dance so hard for me? Why can't I seem to get the rhythm of Your dance? Why do You....well, why don't You just....why don't You just walk away and find another partner? I'm sure there are others who will catch on quicker. Besides, I'm growing weary."

"Rest in Me. Let Me lead. Relax. I don't want to find another partner. I'm staying."

"Surely others can learn quicker, some who have an inclination to rhythm that I don't have."

Your Father is silent. You stop talking and decide to let Him lead.

Finally, He speaks. "Every time your feet get under My feet, you learn something about My Nature. Every time. Lessons about Me often come through pain. That's because your human nature always screams out to be in control, to do the leading, to make all the decisions. Letting Me lead is not something that is natural. It's a conscious choice, a stubborn choice, made even as your self-nature screams out to be in control."

You listen. You ponder His words. You put your head on His large chest and listened to the soothing beat of His heart. You feel light. Your feet move easily over Life's dance floor. An encouraging thought works its way from your heart into your mind. You remember something.

Each time your feet get in His way, and your toes get stepped on, you feel, at the very same instant, a tightening of His arms around your body. The rhythm of that understanding emerges. Each time your toes get in His way, a definite pulling of your life toward His life takes place, as if a delightful law of the universe is that when God allows pain, He also then tightens His arm of love. Yes, that is it! *That* is it! Your body now becomes even more relaxed, and you are aware that the steps between the moves are clearer and sharper. One more noticeable thing: You seem to know which way Your Father is headed. No more guessing. No more trying to keep up with His leading.

Not that you can read His mind, but you feel a strange oneness with Him—a unity. You cling to Him more tightly, sensing that without Him on the floor of Life with you, obvious disaster will occur, yet your clinging feels differently now.

You hold on to His arms, giving in to the music, as if this is what you are created to do! Meant to do! This is where you belong, exactly where you belong! Why has it taken you so long to understand?

"Will my feet ever get under yours again, Father? Is stepping on my toes a thing of the past?"

"That's entirely up to you."

You think about that for a few minutes, then you say, "Well, I suppose it's okay if it does happen again. If that's what it takes to stay on the dance floor with you, I suppose it's okay."

The evening continues. You have never known such contentment. Nothing disturbs you now. Yes, there are sounds in the background. Yes, there are distractions that will take you away from your commitment to the dance, but being with Him is all that seems to matter right now. You close your eyes and think of all those you want to know this same peace. Family members dash through your mind. Old friends. Church folks still living in denial of truth. They have to know. They have to hear about this glorious tranquility.

Finally, after a long silence, your Father speaks once more. "I'm pleased with how you are learning. We can now go deeper. We will go deeper together into life."

"But," you say, "I want to remain like this with you forever."

You wonder what had made the difference in you. What is it that moved you from being sloppy in the dance to being able to move with the rhythm?

Your Father reaches over to lovingly touch your face. "When did it all change? You don't know?"

"No, I don't know!"

"Why it changed the minute you started moving in the dance *with* Me, instead of pulling *against* Me. It changed when you submitted and let Me truly lead. It changed when you began to love My dance *more than anything*."

You smile. "I do love Your dance, Father. I really do. I don't even know when it happened. I just know I never want to be without you again. It is worth going through sore toes to get to this place of harmony with you. How could You tell? When could You tell?

What exactly did I do to move over from my side to Yours?"

Your Father smiles. "What did you do? You don't know? You really aren't aware?"

"No."

"You changed, My beloved, when you forgot about yourself and started humming with Me. When that happened, you forgot about figuring everything out. You forgot about yourself. Your heart began to naturally follow. When your heart followed, your feet followed. It all changed for you when you started to hum along with Me. Moving with Me became the natural thing to do. I knew then that you loved My dance."

You take a deep breath, move a little closer to His heart, and notice how the beats of your heart seemed to match His. Softly, you join Him as He hums. Gratefully, you continue His dance, feeling sure your toes will get stepped on again but knowing as they do, at the same time, you will experience His lovingly strong grip.

To My Reader: Submitting to God's leadership is difficult and sometimes painful. Letting go of control is hard. As we submit our will to His, something beautiful happens inside of us. We were never meant to lead God. What about you? Are you ready to allow Him to be the leader in this dance? Can you be a follower now? If you would like to talk to your Father about it, I would love to offer a prayer.

Prayer: Dear Father, you know me best, and you know I like to be in control. I have a list of things to do each day; I have people to check on, projects to complete, and places to go. Please help me know how I can dance this dance and allow you to be in control. I really do want to go on the dance floor of life with you tonight. Help me to trust your leadership and to let go of my control. In Jesus' Name, Amen

Chapter Eight

Fast Dance

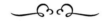

Most of us have been doing a fast dance ever since we were born. Days and nights zoom past us, and often we comment "How time flies!" And, it does. With life's demanding schedule, we all live in the fast track. Yesterday got caught up in the traffic of busy jobs and busy families. Today got caught up in the continuing move of getting ourselves and everybody else where we needed to be. We relax so seldom that our vacations almost seem uncomfortable to us, an intrusion. It's hard to put down the cell phone, turn off the fax machine, and simply slow down. Maybe you can understand the following scenario. Read this story about you. Maybe it *is* you, or someone you know.

Even before I was born, I was moving. After I was born, from that time on, I never stopped moving. My arms moved fast. My legs moved fast. My mouth moved fastest of all. Unless I was asleep, my mouth puckered, twitched, smiled, yawned or opened wide for food. I couldn't wait to do more, so as soon as I could, I began crawling. Soon afterwards, I began walking, then trotting, then running, and I never stopped. I ran everywhere I went. It felt wonderful. I couldn't imagine walking any other way but fast.

As I grew older, I was either running from or to something. I ran from fears, imaginations, hollow dreams and enemies. I ran to a dance, to a football game and to soccer. Later, I ran to keep up with my friends' accomplishments, to keep away from my parents'questions, to try to be first and the very best. I ran forward to start a career and even further to make money. I ran to find the one I wanted to marry, to raise a family and to buy a home. I ran to find the abundant life but never did. Then I reached middle age.

I kept running, and now the race seemed even more important. I ran to fight for my political views and to fight against those who differed with me. I ran to lose weight, to keep up with my friends' fine houses, and to spend more money. I ran to own more than one car, a boat, and a house on the lake. I ran to provide for my children, to pay car and house insurance, and to buy the very best for those I loved. I ran to have the prettiest, the nicest, and the most expensive. I still ran to find the abundant life but never found it. Instead, I ran smack into old age.

I kept running. Now, my body wouldn't run as fast, but I couldn't stop running in other ways. I ran looking back to see what I had missed in my youth. I ran to make sure I didn't miss anything from my middle age years. I ran to show my adult children that I was still in the game. I ran looking for my losses. I ran against those old friends whose ideas differed from mine. I ran toward those old friends whose ideas agreed with mine. I ran to play cards, to take care of grandchildren. I ran to show others that I could still run, and to show the younger generation that I would still be somebody good to have around. Sadly, I never ran into the abundant life.

I guess I'll be running until I die. It will be then that I will finally be completely still enough to enjoy the abundant life. Too still. Dead still. Unfortunately, it will be too late.

As I make that fly into my heavenly home, I'll probably wonder. Will I look back over my shoulder, wondering where all the time went? Will I wonder why I never was able to slow down? Will I wonder if the rat race really even mattered? Will I remember past accomplishments as worth all the trouble? Will I wish there had been more time simply to stop? As I glide through heaven's doors, will I be content to sit on rainbows and dangle my feet on the clouds? Will slowing down produce joy for me? In that land where I never have to run again, will I even know how to appreciate it?

The God of heaven is the same God of earth. He is God of all, God Almighty! The God who wants you to stop the Fast Dance will be the same God who waits for you in heaven. He wants you to learn now, while you still can, that there is a Slow Dance. There is a dance that frees you from all of the anxious days and nights of your youth, middle age, and old age.

It's not a lazy dance, a too-slow dance that doesn't call for your very best. It's not an unrealistic dance, a don't-look-at-reality dance. It's not a denial dance. It's simply a slower dance from the one you now know. It's a dance of love, a dance that captures the moment, photographs it in frames of beauty, and soothes your weary heart with tranquility. If you ever want to know anything about the abundant life, you must stop to know the author of this dance. He made up all the steps, and He is the only one who can teach you. Listen to an invitation to His Slow Dance.

"Seek Me," He calls. "Seek Me in your inner life, your relationships, your financial situations! Value right living! Flee from anything that leads you astray! The Taste of Success, if mixed with the Drink of Scheme, will lead to your destruction. I will supply all you will ever need. I never run dry. I always have fresh nourishment for you. Seek me above all else. When you run the race of life, you always lose something of value! Only run in one direction. Run to me. Run to my arms of love!"

He continues. "The fruit of righteousness will be peace, the effect of righteousness will be quietness and confidence forever. My people will live in peaceful dwelling places, in secure homes, in undisturbed places of rest." (Isaiah 32: 17-18)

There's more. He looks straight at you and says, "Stand at the crossroads and look; ask for the ancient paths, ask where the good way is, and walk in it, and you will find rest for your souls." (Jeremiah 6:16)

The choice is clearly yours. You can choose the abundant life now, the life of peace and rest. Your

Father God knows how to show you. He will lead you to those paths of righteousness, but you must take His hand and accept His invitation.

Suddenly, from across the Dance Floor, you see the Son. He is searching for someone. He moves with the rhythm of the dance the same way your Father God does. He has the same look about Him, a look of love and kindness resting brilliantly, yet serenely, on His face.

The Son spies you and calls in His kindest voice, "Come unto me, all ye who are weary and burdened, and I will give you rest." (Matthew 11:28)

The call is compelling and refreshing. How wonderful it would be to just go to Him now, to go to Him and find rest. In the middle of running everywhere, this rest sends a sweet perfume of love into your weariness. What would it take to answer this call? What would you have to give up? What would you do with your many jobs, your obligations, your commitments? Is there truly a way to let go of running here, running there and, abandoning all, run straight to His arms? How will you ever know if you don't give it a try? Do you even dare?

Who or what is keeping you from this kind of total abandonment? Who is keeping you from this commitment? No matter what any man has done to you, this is one answer that can be blamed on no one but yourself. *You are the reason* you can't commit to God. Another's hurt might have torn your heart out, broken it in two, and left you for dead. Someone in your life might have done all he could to make your life miserable, but no one can keep you from finding your own peace with God. No one can keep you from recognizing your rightful place as God's daughter!

You are invited to a Father-Daughter Dance in your honor! You are invited to allow your Father God to love away all of those hurts, as He pours His healing kisses into your wounds. You are invited to stop the fast dance and participate in the slow dance, allowing your Father God to securely hold you close on life's dance floor. You are invited, so why is acceptance so hard to do?

Perhaps you blame your heavenly Father for things in your life you couldn't understand. Maybe you've let weeds of anger and resentment towards God choke out His peace. Maybe you've even tried to go the "religious" route before, only to end up in more confusion as new hurts came along.

You might think that a relationship with your Father God is only for the weak. You are strong, after all! You'd have to be, you tell yourself, in order to survive your life!

Maybe pride keeps you from asking Him for help. You don't want to admit that you can't handle life, and so you refuse to invite help from the author of Life! You might even think that your friends and family view you as the strong person, and you would let them down if you admitted you needed help. You rather like being thought of as capable and strong, and you want nothing to tarnish that image.

Often we simply cannot accept that God really can make changes in our lives. We look aimlessly for those outer changes, the ones that will change "the other person." We pray and plead, "If only you will change him, then I will...." We focus on another's problems rather than on our own problems. We'll try to get repaired if he gets repaired, but please—him first!

You will only sink deeper into depression, though, if you wait for that to happen. It might. It might not. If you're praying that way, keep on praying, but pray first for yourself. There are many documented answers to prayers stapled to the bulletin boards of heaven!

However, I don't think God cares too much for "tag-him-first, and-then-tag-me" prayer demands. God wants you to recognize *your* need, *your* call to His heart, *your* invitation to dance. He has so much to share with you on the dance floor. There is so much He longs to tell you about His plans for you! Of course, He is interested in those you bring before Him. He's God! He cares about that other one just as much as He cares about you, but He has His own methods and timetable, and He's been moving in those same methods ever since time began. Other than your prayers, He doesn't need your help. Take care of yourself and your relationship with Him. Leave all others to Him! Ouch!

Sure, that other person may have been doing all the "bad stuff!" He may be the one who needs a miracle! No matter. The principle still applies. Take him to your Father and leave him there. Then get out there on the dance floor and learn what your Father God wants to teach you! He's not finished yet with you.

Right now, what He wants to tell you is this. If the fast dance of life has kept you in knots, running here, running there, it is time for a change. Only you can make the change. There may be some circumstances and events over which you have no control. Whether those outward circumstances change or not, the inner you has great reason to celebrate! There is a ball in your honor, and it's starting right now.

Do you hear the band getting their instruments ready? Can you see the soundman putting the equipment in place? Look at the table decorations. Flowers, candles and glitter highlight the center of each table. Look closely at the picture in the heart shaped frames in the center of each table. It's your picture! Everyone is coming to honor you! They will watch with great admiration as you dance first, then second, then every dance with your Father. All of the dances are "no break" dances, so He doesn't plan to let you go all night long. He doesn't plan to share you with anyone else!

What kind of gown will you wear? Silk, taffeta or velvet? What color? Have you slipped on your dancing shoes yet? Get ready. He's walking toward you now. See the loving smile on His face? Is your heart beating wildly? Your Father God is coming to take you onto the dance floor of life.

The band is ready. Everyone is in place. As you slip your hands in His, the music begins. What sort of dance will begin your elegant ball? Don't you know? Of course you do. It's a Slow Dance. You never have to dance a fast dance again. Rest. Relax. Claim righteousness as your cover and peace as your guard.

After all, you were never meant for the fast dance. It's slow dancing from here on out!

To My Reader: Are you tired of the fast dance you've known most of your life? Have you ever just wanted to stop the band and move into a slow dance? We seem to thrive on movement, but your Father longs for you to know about His Slow Dance. He wants to take your hand and help you enjoy a slower pace. Why don't you ask Him to help you?

Prayer: Father, I do want to slow down my life's fast pace. I don't know how. I need your help. Please take me to the Dance Floor of Life and teach me about your Slow Dance. In your Name I pray. Amen.

Chapter Nine

Eve's Dance
(To Help You See Why You Do What You Do)

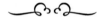

Why is life so hard? Why do we fall all over ourselves with one bad choice after another? What about temptation? Why can't we control those areas that hide secretly inside, waiting for another chance to bring us down? Why do we have such a hard time with our temper? Why do we struggle with forgiveness? Why can't we be, if not perfect, closer to perfect than we are?

What does an ancient garden found in the book of Genesis, two people, one tree and a snake have to do with you and me? Why is there, existing somewhere in our subconscious, a strong familiarity to Eve? We feel like we know that woman! She's kin! We could be her! Well, actually, we are her!

God created Eve and invited her to His dance, but Eve rebelled and chose her own moves. We are often lured to dance Eve's dance. We wish we didn't like her music, but the truth is we do.

Like Eve, we want to call the shots, control the events in our garden home, and convince our husbands that we are right. We are Eve in that we want to test the parameters given to us, and in our vulnerability we would never understand all of the consequences that would occur as a result of our poor choices.

She and Adam get all the blame for original sin, but if you and I had been there that day, we would have, at the serpent's bidding, eaten the fruit with her. We are, therefore, co-conspirators in the fall and in the doctrine of original sin. Together, we would have bitten into the pleasing-to-the-eye appeal of the fruit, already wondering if some other woman in some other garden had a tree any prettier than ours. Our minds would quickly jump toward being the first women to patent fruit decorations for our kitchens, as dollar signs danced through our heads!

If sin entered Eve at this time, then sin entered me as well, and from that momentary decision to eat the fruit and disobey God, Eve and I became a part of fallen humanity, completely helpless to return to our former state. Together we would have marched over to Adam, telling him to take a bite, while we were probably inwardly lauding over him our prideful recognition that he was made only from dust, while we were made from solid bone of his rib.

When sin entered our human situation, life started to spiral downward. Nothing would be easy. Satan began his claim on human life and his energetic battle to warp our minds and souls. Jealousy, hatred, war, lust and every other evil invaded the human race, causing pain, havoc and death. I know this story well because I partake in the fight daily. Don't you?

Quite often, as negative habits or wrong choices find their way into my heart, I hear this loud noise in my ear. A crunching, munching sound. It's Eve, chewing that which was forbidden by God. She offers me another piece of fruit. I'm tempted! More often than not, I want to join her. (Well, truthfully, I am not that fond of fruit. But, if there had been a chocolate tree in that garden....)

Then, I think of her first dance on earth, her dance with the devil. Even though the devil had never had dance lessons, Eve chose to dance with him! It was her biggest mistake! He even wined her and dined her in preparation for the dance, using enticing words that undermined God's directions.

Satan misquoted God to Eve. "You must not eat from any tree in the garden?" (Genesis 3:1) God had not said that. He had said not to eat from the tree of the knowledge of good and evil because if they did, they would surely die. (Genesis 2:16-17) He got Eve so confused that she then added to God's word.

She said to Satan, "We may eat fruit from the trees in the garden, but God did say 'You must not eat fruit from the tree that is in the middle of the garden, and you must not touch it or you will surely die!'" (Genesis 3:2) Actually, God never said anything about not touching a tree.

So, where was God as all hell began to break loose? Since God is all knowing, nothing about any of this caught Him off guard. Contrary to what it may sometimes appear, this truly is God's world. He really is on the Throne and knows all things. Satan may have entered a snake and brought temptation and ultimate downfall, but God wasn't hiding behind another tree in that garden, shaking in fearful anticipation of the choice Eve would make. Rather, He places Himself in the position of desiring fellowship with us, while at the same time allowing the Enemy to do his dirty work. It's a risk, but He takes that risk, hoping that our heart's longings will cause an even greater heart's hunger for Him. Then, the fellowship would be two-sided, mutual, and indescribably significant.

While God presents Himself to us through the pages of the Bible as the one true God, worthy of our praise and reverence, He also comes to us as a God of tender mercy and compassion. God wants us to be comfortable with the image we have of Him as Father. He cares greatly for us, and He constantly reaches out to do things for us.

I believe God adores his daughters, and we would probably turn red from embarrassment over how many times He speaks of us to His angels. He delights when we sit down to talk to Him, or to listen to Him tell us stories of how much we mean to Him. I think He would go to the ends of the earth to work things out for our good.

You and I bring a smile to His lips every morning we awake, and when we go to sleep at night, He decides to stay awake to watch over us. In my own life, there have been many times when He came to me and sat down by me when I cried. He's held me when I thought life couldn't go on, and when I have been tempted to wallow in despair, He has sent a love note to me through a friend or family member. I've found personal love notes from Him in the pages of the Bible. He always helps me feel better. I guess you could say He spoils me.

As soon as Satan began to smile over his victory in the Garden, God pulled out His Plan B. He would win mankind back through a covenant plan, with specific directions for implementation beginning in Genesis and continuing through Revelation. God had to tell His story, and so He chose to tell it through Abraham and his descendants. In an effort to do something about the sinful state mankind was now in, the shedding of blood was necessary. God initiated the sacrifice of animals. The plan is laid out in such vivid detail that I grow weary in reading the effort that God went through to get us back.

A detailed explanation was given to Moses so that the Hebrew people would know what to do to atone for their sins. The meaning of the atonement is that man's spirit can be restored into harmony with God. (Oswald Chambers *Bringing Sons Into Glory*, page 76, Christian Literature Crusade, Fort Washington Pennsylvania, 1943)

Over and over again, these sacrifices had to be made because after each sacrifice and each atonement, sinful men and women continued to be who they were, fallen humanity going on a continual downward plunge. Then, God put into effect His very best plan of all. After hundreds and hundreds of years of animal sacrifices, He ended this period with one final sacrifice, but it wasn't an animal that was sacrificed this time. God knew that the only way to give us the victory over sin was for Him to come to earth and die Himself.

True to his nature of being a risk-taker, God came as a baby, was born to a woman and was given an earthly father. He had sisters and brothers, worked for a living, and got hungry. He needed to stop and rest just like everybody else in his family. Everything He did had the soft scent of heaven's love mingled with the sweaty smell of human toil. Divinity jumped into humanity, and for a season of thirty-three years, God walked among us in physical form. He showed us love and compassion. Through stories that grab our attention with their simplicity, yet carry such depth that we're still not really sure we are catching on, He places before us new dimensions of thinking and acting. He says some hard things to swallow, and leaves us searching for answers in some areas, while giving us freedom to question, think and gain His ideas for ourselves.

God, through Jesus, doesn't make us obey, but His invitation is so compelling that over two thousand years later, we still want to hear His stories and listen to His teachings. We are fascinated by a God who would come to earth for the purpose of dying.

Being uncomfortable with what we don't understand, we continue on a quest to figure it all out. We always want to come back to that garden, however, where the forbidden fruit grows plentifully on a tree. Our daily inclination is to just go ahead and get another piece! Nothing seems to be working for us anyway! Why not just sink our teeth into its flavor! The tempting fruit has different colors and shapes, various enticing flavors. It hangs from the tree looking like lust, murder, anger, hatred, and any other lie the devil tries to conceal. On the outside, it looks good. On the inside there is a pull straight to hell.

Our lives battle the two struggles within, and with each crunch of sin, we cannot believe how big our Father God is! He created a fruit tree and then died because that fruit harmed his children! Amazing!

Jesus came and died for us so that we could walk past any fruit tree of temptation and know that we do not have to partake! Satan's power over us was defeated at the cross! Just as you and I were in the garden with Eve, we were likewise at Golgotha with Jesus. It was supposed to be us on that tree, not Him! Remember that your name is engraved on the palm of His hand, engraved there before you were even born. Jesus stopped often on that hot, dusty day just to look at your name as He walked the hill to His death. On every turn of the road on that journey, He stopped a second to think of you and smile.

You kept him going. You were the reason He died! He would do anything for you! If you had actually been there and tried to take his place, He wouldn't have let you. He wanted to do it for you. He wanted all of your sin to be placed upon Him so that through His death, He might pay your penalty.

I cannot comprehend that kind of love, but I don't have to. He will be satisfied not to explain, only for me to receive. In my feeblest efforts to make sense out of His death, I conclude with this one unbelievably uplifting thought: I am no longer under that curse of the tree. I owe God something for that, after all, because the curse is a great stumbling block in my life, but He doesn't make me pay. He did it for me, and He did it all almost two thousand years before I was even born!

Although, I no longer had the inability to escape sin, I still had one big fear. Death. What a wonderful surprise Jesus gave to me when He didn't stay in the grave! He showed me that I, too, would live beyond the grave, and that death was not my enemy. That's incredibly good news for a woman who used to be afraid of the dark.

When I was a little girl, I often wondered how Jesus could get small enough to live in my heart, and as I've grown older, I realize that He never did get *small enough*. He was *big enough* to want to live in my heart. He does this through the reality of the Holy Spirit dwelling inside of me! It's a divine mystery, a humbling fact, a glorious union.

The only way that I can stop being pulled to Eve's disposition is to allow the disposition of Jesus Christ to take over inside of me! That's what I really want, deep down in my soul. Every morning when I start my day, I need to remind myself that no matter how much I want to appear to have everything all together, I am just one step away from that fruit tree. As I awake, my ears may hear the alarm clock, but my nose is busy doing something else. It's busy sniffing, hunting the scent of forbidden fruit. Thank God that because of Jesus' death, I can taste of Him instead of that fruit and see that He is good! Still, when temptations rise to meet me, as they always will, I recognize Eve's familiar voice in my ear, saying things similar to what she said to Adam. Those compelling words of Eve's Dance come back to me over and over.

"Go ahead. Do it. Try it. You'll like it! Who will know? What's so bad about it, anyway?"

Is that you again, Eve?

To My Reader: Maybe you tire of realizing the constant negative pull on your life. You are all too aware of your propensity to sin, the way you *do* what you don't want to do and don't do what you really *want* to do. It is who we are, our nature, our kinship with all humanity. However, this nature does not have to reign in your life. That nature does not have to win. You do not have to become sin's slave. Jesus broke that bondage over you. When you get up in the morning and say, "Is that *you* again, Eve?" call out to the Lord and say, "I need *You* again, Jesus." He will lift the power of sin. You are not a captive any more.

Prayer: Dear Jesus, great Bondage-Breaker, free me from the sin that pulls my life down. Make me a captive only of you. Enslave me to your love, your will, your ways. I want to be totally yours. In your Name I pray, Amen.

Chapter Ten

Dance of Honor

Your Father God wants to take you to the dance floor, treating you with great honor and respect. He has a loving opinion of you. He regards you highly. He values you. He respects you, even though you might feel you've done nothing to earn that respect. He looks upon you as who you are in His eyes, not the eyes of anyone else. He views you in light of how He made you to be, not what you have become. Your Father sees you through His highest plans for you, even if those plans haven't even begun to show forth in your life. He thinks only the best about you, not the worst. He believes in you.

Don't fear that He might know too much dirt on you to love you. He knows all the dirt on you and loves you anyway. Even though you've acted like a spoiled brat from time to time, He places the highest honor imaginable on you when He calls you His daughter. No matter that you have a few secret sins that nobody else knows about, He wants to hold your hand and take you to the dance floor. Even if what you have done is disgusting, awful, and completely terrible, He makes no apologies to others on the floor when He walks out with you. He does not feel He has to make excuses for you. He's not ashamed to be seen in public with you. When you walk out onto the floor, it doesn't matter to Him if others begin whispering gossip from one table to the next. He doesn't care. He doesn't notice. He only notices you. He has no concerns, except one.

He is concerned about your hurt. He knows there are others who haven't treated you with the honor you deserve, and He doesn't like that. He realizes you have been hurt by some who meant it and some who didn't. He sees deep into your inner emotional pool, and what others have done to you brings Him pain. He sees injustice, indifference, disrespect, and misplaced anger. When He looks at your insides, He sees all of those pains stirring around. They stir in your stomach, in your intestines and in your heart. As this happens, each organ becomes tense. Each stir causes a fresh pain. Tears start deep inside, joining the unhealthy stir and finally making their way to your tear ducts.

Everything has not always been your fault. You've made your share of mistakes, sure, but the way you feel right now is not completely your fault. There are hidden reasons that have been sitting unnoticed inside of you for a long time. Maybe you never wanted to look at those feelings. You don't want to even think about them. You'd like very much to close your eyes and never deal with them. You're not even really sure what all of them are. Every now and then, you look inside, and you know. You know that until those things are dealt with, you will never feel worthy or useful or productive.

Unfortunately, dealing with them causes you so much turmoil. You try to pull those thoughts out sometimes, and you end up more confused than ever. Besides, you've lived this way for so long now that you don't even recognize truth. You don't recognize reality. You don't recognize the woman you wanted to be but never could become. You used to know that dream, but the dream has gotten lost. So, here you are, frozen in an emotional state of not knowing which way to turn. You are accustomed to turning the way others want you to. You are accustomed to letting others do most of your thinking. You are accustomed to not making waves. The woman you wanted to be is hiding somewhere between a truth and a lie, and no one but you can decide which of those two sides will win.

Up walks your hero, your Father God, and He continues His invitation to the Dance of Honor. Hesitantly, you accept but you don't know the steps. What if you mess up? After all, your partner is God. You don't want anyone noticing your mistakes.

"What about your efforts," your Father asks? "What if they notice your efforts? Let's turn this around. You are so used to thinking negatively about yourself that you cannot imagine thinking the opposite way. I want to show you how."

You begin walking to the Dance, but you feel so heavy. A huge rock is tied to your foot. Another rock appears on one of your arms. Another is tied around your neck.

"What in the world is going on? I can't dance with these heavy weights. I can't even walk. What am I supposed to do with these things? Where did they come from?" you ask.

"They are called burdens," He replies.

"But why did you put them there when you know I can't move with them on me?"

"I didn't."

"Then who did?"

"You did."

"Me? How? I didn't even see any large rocks like this when I came in. I didn't bring in any rope, either."

"You did have the rocks and you had the ropes to tie them with. You just didn't see them. They had become a part of you in such a way that you were used to them. They move everywhere you move. Even when you sleep, they are in the bed with you."

"I'm lost. This is crazy. Rocks. Ropes. Crazy. I want them off!"

"So do I. Want me to show you how?"

"Yes. How? What do you have to do to get them off of me?"

"Nothing."

"Nothing?"

"That's right. Nothing. I don't have to do anything at all. You do, though."

"Well, if you'll find me a pair of scissors, I'll be happy to cut the rocks free."

"Scissors won't work. The rocks will leave when you hand them to me."

"You're kidding, right? You want me to just hand them to you and they'll be gone? That sounds way too easy."

"You pick up the one from around your arm first. Then, you will have both arms free to take off the others." It's a struggle. You can't get it to budge.

"It's so heavy. It feels like something is in here."

"It is."

"What?"

"I'll name a few. This rock carries *circumstances* you can't solve and *people* that you cannot change. Remember that problem you've been worrying about? It's in there. You've also had a financial strain lately. It's in there. You're not sure what to do about a certain situation, and you've been agonizing over it. That's in there, too. Then there's that person at work."

"Will you help me get it off?"

"Glad to. Just hand it to me."

"I can't. It's too heavy for me."

"That's only because you're really not ready to get rid of it. You've had this rock so long that you're not sure how to live without it. If you truly want it gone, then you have to decide you won't take it back."

"TAKE IT BACK? Who in their right mind would do such a thing?"

"Humans. Every morning. Every afternoon. Every night."

"Well, I can answer for this human. I will give it to you and not take it back."

"Great. Try again."

Easily the stone slides off your arm and you hand it to your Father. It is no longer heavy. Then He does a strange thing. He places it on His arm.

"Why are you doing that?"

"I'll tell you later."

"Well, what's in the one on my leg?"

"That one carries *attitudes* you've held on to for a long time. Anger. Unforgiveness. Hurt feelings. Gossip spread about you. Tears."

"I definitely want this one gone. I promise I won't take it back."

"Try that last sentence again. I've had a lot of dealings with humans. Probably it would be best only to say 'I will TRY not to take it back."

"I'll try."

The rock slips off you, as if it had oil under it.

"Whew. That feels much better." You hand it to your Father and He ties it to His leg.

"One more. What's in this one around my neck? It's pulling me. I want it off, and I will try not to take it back."

"You're catching on. This one is filled with *your past*. You did some things you regret and yet can't let go. You hurt some people. Some people hurt you. This one holds any pain you had as a child or adult when you were neglected, put aside and made to feel you were an intrusion into someone's world. In this rock you carry not only the feeling of being a disappointment and in the way of someone, but also the fear that you will be a disappointment to somebody else."

"I don't want this rock. It is hanging around me like a noose. It feels like it's strangling me."

"It is. It has been. It always will unless you can hand this rock to me."

"I can. I want to, and I will try not to take it back. Ever."

Your Father takes this last rock from you and slips it over His head.

"Come on. Let's go out there now to the Dance of Honor."

You feel anything but honor right now, but you do feel some relief. Great relief. Your steps are light, your arm is free, and your neck is marvelously released. Suddenly, you think of your Father and you stop.

"What about you? I didn't even think about you. I was so busy thinking of how I could be free from these horrible burdens I've been carrying. Now you have them. Now you are hurting. I'm so sorry. I don't want you to hurt while you dance."

Your Father smiles and takes your hand as He begins to lead you in the Dance of Honor.

"My daughter, those burdens are now mine. You've handed them to me. They aren't yours any more unless you choose to take them back. They are heavy on you. They feel like a feather on me. I honor you by loving you into knowing me and by taking away your burdens. I honor you by showing you how to live without the pain you have been carrying. You are too important to me for these burdens to hold you down forever. I cherish the person I created you to be. I honor the bright shining star inside of you, the star that has been hurt by the wounds of life. I want you to be free."

You don't understand. You've never had someone love you this much. You've never had someone take hurts from you like this. All over your body you feel wonderful, free, joyful, very content and very honored. You feel special and loved.

"Cast your cares on me. I care for you. I am faithful. I will keep these now. After this dance is finished, you will continue to feel lighter than you have in years. The only way that won't happen is if you take them back."

"I won't," you answer. "I prom...."

He smiles and looks lovingly into your eyes. "Remember who you're talking to. If you do, I'll be the first to know."

You like His smile and the warmth of His hand and even the sense of humor He allowed you to have in this conversation. What an incredibly wonderful day this has been. As the music ends, you really want to stay, but you know you have to go. You have to see if the freedom is still there at work tomorrow, or in your home or as you visit with your friends.

You are sure it will be. You know it will be. You can prom.... well, you can try with everything in you to leave these burdens with your Father. Why has it taken so long for you to realize that His love is truly this great for you? Why has it taken you this long to give up those burdens you held? Why has it taken you so long to trust Him with them?

In release and trust comes blessed freedom. Hallelujah for a Father who loves you this much. A sense of His respect for you fills your heart. You are special to Him. He values you. He honors you. The God of the Universe honors *you*. It's more than you can take in.

You hold your shoulders straight and begin His dance. You feel light for the first time in years. He actually chooses for you to place your burdens on His shoulders. Without them, this dance moves gracefully over the dance floor. You could stay here forever.

To My Reader: Maybe you can ask yourself the same question. Is there something bothering you today? Why has it taken so long to turn your burden over to the only One who can handle them? Would you like to do that now? If you need a prayer, I would love to give you one.

Prayer: Dear Father, I am consumed with something, and I cannot seem to move past it. It loads me down, and I have no peace or joy. I want to hand it over to you. I don't want it any more. Please give me the strength to leave it with you. Thank you that you are the burden bearer. Thank you that you honor me by choosing to lift the weight of this burden, so that I can be free. I am so grateful. By an act of trust and faith, I am handing it to you now. In your Son's Name I pray, AMEN.

Chapter Eleven

Dance of the Overflowing Cup
(The Shepherd's Dance)

The music begins, but you don't want to listen. You have just gone through a difficult time in your life. No one knows how hard it has been. Outwardly, you continue to smile, but your insides are shattered. Getting out of bed in the morning is a struggle. Moving into the day's tasks seems insurmountable. You do not want to dance. You would feel much better not to be noticed, to sit behind others and just watch. You purposefully pull your chair to the back of the room and seclude yourself behind a large group of folks. You want the pain to hide behind the mask of your "I'm just fine" face. Talking about this would bring tears. You close your eyes, trying to block out the tremendous hurt of your life, the unwanted circumstances that have held your heart in prison. Something unexpected soon happens.

You feel a presence behind you, and you know immediately who it is. Your Father God walks softly, but His presence is like none other. Can you deny your Father's request to dance? Can you tell Him you don't have the energy to get on the Dance Floor of Life today? Will He understand? How can He? Even your Father God doesn't live inside your own particular disappointments, the injuries thrown at you by life's circumstances, the cruelty of humans to other humans, especially those that have hit you as their target. He is, after all, God. How could He even relate?

He offers His hand and you refuse. He stands beside you silently, looking at you and waiting. You intend to win. You won't go. He can't make you.

He speaks. "No, I can't make you. You have the right to choose, but something waits for you in this dance. Something you will miss if you don't come with Me. You don't have to do anything but get up and try. All you have to do is follow as I lead. Think about it."

You don't have to think. You already know. This is too embarrassing. You know some of the people at the dance. They will see your tears and plastered-on smile. You know you cannot hide this from some of your friends. No, it's better to sit this one out. You tell God you just cannot.

Then, Your Father God does a strange thing. He pulls up a chair and sits down beside you. His towering presence makes you appear tiny. That's okay. You already feel insignificant. You wonder why He even bothers. You look over at His face. It is full of kindness. Still, you are adamant. You won't go on the Dance Floor of Life today.

Hours pass. God waits. He never leaves. You want to get up, but actually you are enjoying the sound of the music, so you decide to stay. Something is extraordinary about this music. It's restful. You feel yourself relaxing. Your jittery stomach lets go of its twisted knot and peace enters. You look at your Father. Doesn't He have something better to do? Doesn't He have thousands of other women who need Him? Why does He insist on staying by your side?

Finally, He asks, "How are you feeling now? Is there a chance I might have this next dance?"

There's something endearing about the way He asks, something so appropriate, so kind and loving, something courteous, and respectful. You think it over, but making one foot move in the direction of the dance floor seems an impossible task. So, you remain seated. Your Father God remains seated too.

"I am so unhappy, Father. Life is not fair. It seems that no matter how hard I try, things just don't work out for me. Just let me sit this one out. I'm tired of trying."

He answers, "You don't have to do anything in this dance but follow Me. I have some surprises in store for you in this dance, wonderful surprises that will bring you past the turmoil and into comfort. You only need to trust as I lead and you follow."

A few more hours pass. Finally, He speaks again. "Oh, and you are wrong about thinking I cannot relate. Have you forgotten I lived on earth through

Jesus, My Son for thirty-three earth years? There is no pain, sadness or heartache that you experience that I have not known. I've lived it. I can relate. I know all about it."

Your body is so relaxed that you decide you can get up. "I can't promise I will stay, though."

"I understand. You don't have to go out there alone. Here, take My hand."

It is the most remarkable hand you've ever held. Strength surges from His hand to yours, and you feel unbelievably secure.

He begins His dance, holding you close to His chest. The security you felt in His hand continues. You don't know why you fought this so many hours. Peace saturates you when you remain this close to your Father God. You close your eyes and wonder if simply being in His Presence could remove every pain on earth. All your worries suddenly seem insignificant.

You open your eyes when you feel something against your side. A shepherd's staff is resting over His right arm, and in the other hand, He holds a rod. Suddenly, the pains and hurts of your life begin to assault you. You can literally feel them as they attack, but they are unable to reach you. Your Father God takes the rod and fights off your enemies as they appear. You pull away and try to run back to your seat. He takes His staff and puts it around you, gently pulling you back to His arms. It's incredible! How did He do that?

He explains. "You are one of My sheep. I am your Shepherd. The Shepherd watches over His sheep. I will protect you from the onslaught of the enemies that try to take away your peace. There is no need to fear. I will pull you back when you leave My presence."

Now you hear the slow trickle of a stream. The feel of the dance floor changes as under your feet you feel thick, green grass. The color is rich, unlike any green you've ever known before. The water in the brook is the clearest you've ever seen. Your Father God stops dancing and sits down in the thick grass, asking you to join Him. Something about the beauty of the luxuriant grass beckons you to follow. In fact, when you see your Father lie down, you decide you want to do the same.

You wonder how God, who is over all the activities of this world, has time to lie here like this. You realize that if He has time, then surely you do, too. There is no feeling of having to rush to the next task in your life. You cannot even remember your busy "to do" list for this day. Stress melts off your body and onto the grass. The peaceful water mirrors the sun, and in the quietness you cannot even remember what you were so upset about. You could stay here for days! You are so glad He wanted you to lie down in these beautiful green pastures and that He led you beside the still waters. You've never known such tranquility. Nothing matters to you now except following Him.

When the two of you get up, after what seems like hours, you are restored. Hope replaces despair. Joy roots out worry. All of your body and soul is relaxed. To think it all happened because you decided to follow the Shepherd.

Then, you remember your biggest concern, and suddenly it looms once again before you. Does He know? Does He know what the doctor told you?

"Yes, of course I know what the doctor told you. I know that you are afraid of his diagnosis. I know that you think you might be walking through a valley that has a huge shadow over it. It is overwhelming you with its presence. It is the shadow of your death."

"Well, then, why are you putting me through this? If You are who You say You are, and You know my fear of death, why don't You just remove the problem? You can do that, can't you?"

"My daughter, until you are out of this world, you will always walk near the shadow of death. Hearing the doctor's news does not make the reality of death any different. The shadow of death stalks daily over My children, but it's just a shadow. It's not the reality of death. A shadow can loom so large that you think it will swallow you. A shadow's purpose is to bring fear, but it is still only a shadow. It comes from the enemy. All of My children, however, are born with an expiration date. They can go through life *afraid of that date,* or go through life *victorious over that date.*

"Fear is the biggest enemy the Adversary uses against My sheep. Even though you walk with fear through the valley that holds that shadow, your trust in Me will cause you to have no fear. I am with you. I use My rod to fight off the fear that frightens you. I have my staff to pull you to My side when you start to wander inside the dreaded shadow. With me you are safe.

"I love to protect my girls, but some run and hide from Me when they see that shadow. Some close Me out. Still, I stand close by, fighting the enemy of fear with My rod and always drawing My daughters to my side. They may resist, but I don't give up. I want them to come so I can bring them to these waters and this pasture. I'm the only One who can bring them here. They just have to say yes to this dance."

You feel abnormally at peace. You have been handed a diagnosis that could mean the end of your time on this earth, and yet you feel peaceful. A flood of joy rushes all over your body and washes your soul. What is death if God is there? What is fear if God conquers even that?

Your Father holds you as the dance continues. You feel light, relaxed, and free from all fear. He moves you to the other side of the dance floor where a large table awaits. He pulls out a chair for you. It is the only chair there. Quickly you realize this is a large banquet in *your* honor. The table is decorated with garlands of grace and filled with bowls of blessings, packages of peace, and fountains of favor just for you! You see your enemies from afar. They are not invited. They watch but cannot get close to you while you are at this table.

Then the most precious thing happens. Your Father comes behind you and pours something on your head. It is oil. Your spirit surges with a fresh anointing. You are sure you could run any race before you now, conquer every fear known to man, and move in victory through every set-back.

"What is this anointing for, Father?"

His voice carries such authority. "You are anointed for My service. You are anointed so that goodness and mercy will follow you wherever you go. Goodness will give you strength when enemies assail. You will see them as the victims, instead of yourself. Goodness will give you a different way of looking at the heartaches of life. You will look for Me inside the heartaches, and you will find Me."

"Mercy will be your banner. It will go through the storms with you. Mercy will keep everything in perspective. Mercy will take the attention off you and your troubles and place it instead on others, and on Me. Goodness and mercy will follow you all the days of your life. You, my child, will be with Me in My House forever. Starting today, not when your physical body dies, but today. Starting today, you will dwell with Me in high places filled with waters of peace, pastures of comfort, tables of encouragement. All of this is yours if you will allow Me, as your Shepherd, to guide you. I will remove fear. You can live in peace."

You get up from the banquet table, ready to face life once more. This dance has been everything your Father told you it would be. Something is special about this dance. Your doubts have been replaced with new faith. You didn't do anything to receive that faith. It is a gift from your Shepherd. It came as you joined the Shepherd's Dance.

As you head back to your seat, you pick up the large goblet on the table before you. You will take it back as a reminder of this dance and of the peace you can always find when you stay close to your Father. It is filled with all those things He has taught you in this dance. It is filled to the brim. In fact, your cup is overflowing. You decide to put it right by your bed, so that you can drink from it every day.

Problems will come again. Fears will bounce on top of your cup, but they cannot enter. This is the cup of blessings. Hold it tightly. Carry it with you everywhere you go. No matter what the enemy tries to tell you, this is your cup. It overflows with your Father's touch. You feel lighter than you have in years.

He speaks. "When you are feeling low, come back to Me for this dance. We'll dance it again and again. The green pastures and quiet waters will always be here for you. I will always be your Shepherd."

You sit down, a different person than you were before the dance. The blessings are flowing out and over the top of your cup. You smile. How wonderful to know your Father God this way. He is your Father. He is also your Shepherd. You close your eyes now and rest.

To My Reader: When dark nights seem more than you can bear, open your Bible to the twenty-third Psalm and find out what God wants to do for you during your problems. He has a plan for you. If you will allow Him to hand you this overflowing cup, you will walk through life with a different attitude. The overflowing cup reminds you of what is really important.

We don't always get our way, but if we will get out of His way, *He can change our mourning into gladness. He will give you comfort and joy instead of sorrow.* (Jeremiah 31:13)

Prayer: Good Shepherd Father God, thank you that you care too much about me to leave me in despair. You care too much about me to allow me to sit on the sidelines of life and sulk. You intend for me to embrace this Dance of Life with you. You continue to love me into loving you back. Thank you for never giving up on me. In The Good Shepherd's Name, Amen

Chapter Twelve

Real Life Dance

My father was a great storyteller, one who could make my childish heart thrill with excitement. He made up his stories, and laughingly told me as an adult that he never was able to fool me! Whatever his story was, I remembered it and usually remembered that he didn't tell it the same way each time. I was especially fond of the story about the Betty Jo Princess. Each telling was meant to be the same, but my father couldn't remember what he had said the first time. If he had the princess riding on a horse in the story the first time, yet he called the animal a mule the next time, I sat up quickly, reminding him that this wasn't how the story went!

However he told the story, whether he got all of the facts right or not, his purpose remained intact. He wanted to make me think that the Betty Jo Princess was a true story, and that this story was about me! Though I lived in a normal looking home instead of a castle and wore the plain clothes of an ordinary girl, I'm sure I loved thinking about this princess. Because she had my name, well, maybe she could be me! Why not?

I lived most of my young life in the "Why not?" phase. I believed most of what my father said, anyway, so why couldn't I be a real life princess?

I was blessed to live in a home with mature and caring parents. I never knew what it was like to be blamed for something I didn't do, to be told I wasn't worth anything, or to feel that I was in somebody's way. I was very secure, and that security lasted through my high school and college days and ten years into my first marriage.

I wish I could say I didn't take this blessing for granted, but actually I did. So sheltered was I that I had no idea what most of the world was going through. I'm embarrassed to admit now that I thought everybody must have it as good!

Problems in my marriage began to surface in that tenth year. In my naiveté, I thought no one else could possibly have a problem like ours. I retreated into secret pain, choosing not to tell anyone so they would not think less of our marriage or of us. Smiling outwardly, I fought for our survival, feeling on most days that a pain this dark could never be repaired. I saw myself sinking into a deep pit of gloom, danger-ously sitting on neutral with no hope of moving into drive. I hated my appearance, believing that if I were prettier, my husband would still be in love with me. I magnified every physical flaw, and on my self-scoring report card, I received an F.

Even though I've described my father in a truthful way, I did have one problem where he was concerned. I never wanted to disappoint him, and therefore I could not be real with him. I grew up at a time when, as the popular TV series indicated, fathers did know best. At least they thought they did. This daughter would never think otherwise.

Combined with my addictive and unhealthy tendency to please everyone, I worked overtime to make sure I was always in my father's good graces. That's not because he beat me or yelled at me. It was because I cringed when I thought of disappointing him. Therefore, letting my father know about my failing marriage was an impossibility, as far as I was concerned. I was not afraid of him. I was afraid his disappointment in me would hurt us both too deeply. Unfortunately, that didn't make for an honest relationship. I wanted him to remember me always as the Betty Jo Princess.

My husband and I were able to salvage our marriage for the next five years, but trouble surfaced once more. The result was the reality of that very painful word that none of us ever wants to use. Divorce ripped into my family, pulling my husband and me apart and leaving two young sons confused and hurt. I felt terribly guilty that the princess couldn't keep her prince.

I could not talk about it, so I wrote my parents a letter. When a letter came back from my father, I didn't want to open it. I did not think I could handle his hurt. I was in for a surprise. In the letter, he affirmed me over and over again. He let me know how he felt about me as a daughter, mother, and teacher. He bragged on me, saying things I would never have known he even thought! Tears flowed as I read that letter, and along with the tears, I shed something else. I shed my fear of disappointing my earthly father. I lost my fear that I wouldn't please him. Those thoughts had been placed inside of me by my own fears. The way my father felt about me in divorce was the same way he had always felt about me. He hadn't changed his view of me, but I, through this letter, changed my view of him.

God operates in this same way. He has written us love letters, found in the pages of the Bible. In those pages, He tells a story of His great mercy, grace, and compassion for His children. He has never changed how He feels about us. Hopefully, through reading His love letters, we can change our view about Him.

God used the nation of Israel to display His faithfulness. In Scriptures concerning Israel, the truth is the same for Israel as for all those who call Him Father. In Jeremiah, God says "I have loved you with an everlasting love; I have drawn you with loving-kindness." (31:3) Through Isaiah, God says, "Since you are precious and honored in my sight, and because I love you,..." (43:4) Then, again in Isaiah, God says, "Though the mountains be shaken and the hills be removed, yet my unfailing love for you will not be shaken nor my covenant of peace be removed." (54:10)

The Bible is a personal love message from God to you and me. Over and over, God sends out His heart of love.

The psalmist David, in one of his many responses to God's love, says these moving words of thanks to the One who has done so much for him. "O God, you are my God, earnestly I seek you; my soul thirsts for you, my body longs for you, in a dry and weary land where there is no water. I have seen you in the sanctuary and beheld your power and your glory. Because your love is better than life, my lips will glorify you. I will praise you as long as I live, and in your name I will lift up my hands."(Psalm 63:1-4)

The Israelites worshiped God as they said, "He is good; His love endures forever." (2 Chronicles 7:3)

Just as I was the one who placed that imaginary wedge between my earthly father and myself, so we can daily place imaginary wedges between us and our heavenly Father. As we try to avoid disappointing God, we allow those wedges to keep us from being honest with Him.

But, God longs for our honesty. He doesn't make fake promises or false statements to us, and He would like us to respond in the same way. Oddly enough, we fool ourselves into thinking that God doesn't recognize dishonesty! This is God Almighty, the One who knows everything about us! Yet, we sometimes approach Him with cautious lips that smack of being dishonest.

The day came when I had to wake up and realize that the Betty Jo Princess was just a tale made up by my father! Real life struggles quickly took me off my throne and brought me down into reality. I learned to view my earthly father's love in a new way. He had always loved me, no matter what.

My heavenly Father showed me enormous support throughout those difficult years during and after the divorce. I saw Him reach out to me again and again, through His Word, through people, and through circumstances that could not have been orchestrated by human hands. My Father took me on the dance floor of life and showed me that real life is a daily adventure in trusting Him.

After I grew up a bit, I realized I never wanted that other kind of life anyway. The Betty Jo Princess was not able to identify with any one's pain or grief. She wasn't authentic. The real life dance takes me instead, into the hearts of many hurting people, many of whom now walk the road I had to walk many years ago. My Father has been gracious to allow me the chance to pray with and listen to many who now sit where I sat. That's one of His best plans of all. He is a master at taking our grief, wiping our tears, and then sending us forth to help someone else.

I do not believe God caused my divorce, but I do believe He used it to make me real. I had lived in a dream world of "happily ever after." I could never imagine life being so hard, so difficult, so painful as it became through divorce. I'd like to share with you, in a somewhat different form, what God did with my tears. First I need to make it clear that whatever pain I have suffered has been minimal to what so many others have known. I had a lot of help to crawl from below zero, where I sat frozen in helplessness. Others don't have so much help. Still, pain is pain. Now, I can thank God for allowing something to come into my life to make me real.

Growing up, I put on a couple of layers of extra skin. One layer was called *Not me!*, a skin which lived in a dreamland of "Everything is okay. Nothing is wrong with me." The other layer was called *Why me?*, a belief system that could not grasp why anything would go wrong in my life. I don't know a particular time when these extra layers started growing. It was a gradual growth, starting when I was very young. Both skins felt tight next to my original skin, but I didn't even know it. Through the years they became a part of me, and without even realizing they existed, I allowed the layers to grow thicker and thicker.

The skin called *Not me!* was next to my real skin, but it grew so quickly that it practically covered that skin in no time! Looking back, I think I know how *Not me!* first began to grow. Its password was *denial,* and once it unlocked the password, that skin moved in to stay! *Not me!* had no idea of the delusion in which it lived; yet it hid behind its password every day. *Denial* covered for it well. That's why *Not me!* innocently received wrong messages from life.

One of those wrong messages was that things were fine in my life! Living in a fairyland where things were always supposed to turn out right, I never looked beneath the surface of my heart to see if things actually were all right. I simply smiled and moved on to the next thing! I buried any thoughts or concerns. My husband and I were, after all, a model couple, weren't we? How many times had I heard others mention our names, indicating that they hoped they could be as happy as we were. So, we were happy. Weren't we?

I *was* happy, but there definitely were signs that our marriage wasn't happy! Those would go away, I told myself as *denial* covered another day of living in the unreal world of *Not me!*

At some point in my life, I had incorrectly taught myself that, as a Christian, I should always be happy and content! I remember so well my initial inward question as soon as I saw trouble arising in our marriage. I wondered, "How does this pain match up with my concept of Christianity? I thought Christians always smiled. Why can't I smile now?"

My understanding of Christianity took a beating as I questioned my own beliefs. How does a Christian handle this sort of grief, yet remain a "good" Christian? Was it okay with God for me to get really mad about this, or should I simply accept heartache with a *don't worry about me, Lord; I'll be just fine* attitude?

As I explored these questions and others, I was unaware that the skin of *Not me* was getting a bit looser. I was forced to take an honest look at myself, and in the looking, I began to see that my situation had no claim on pain! I saw that Satan targets everyone, including so called "good" Christian women! Slowly, slowly, I began to let others into my hurt. What I saw surprised me! No condemnation. Only sadness from them for me. No judgment. Only grief for my situation. God used these dear people to show me His love. As my unreal view of my life began to fade, the skin of *Not me* started ripping.

The other skin of *Why me*? began intruding on my regular skin early in life, also. Having been brought up in such a secure home environment, I honestly believed I would be kept safe from dangers that others would experience. I know this assumption sounds terribly naive', (and it is!) and I'm embarrassed to admit this now. At that time, I hadn't digested the Bible enough to recognize sin as that stumbling block we all face daily. No one is exempt, even those (or should I say, especially those) brought up in the church.

Why me? bought the lie that bad things can never happen to good people. I felt like I had tried to do the right things, and I did nothing to deserve heartache in my marriage. The question that rang in my ears was *Why should this happen to me?* When I began to really read God's Word, learning that those first followers endured tremendous pain for the gospel, I wanted to crawl into a hole! As I continued opening my wounds to others, they opened theirs to me. I heard story after story of desperate pain. My story was simply one of millions. How could I ever have been so bold as to think I could escape the effect of sin?

Why me? began to loosen and crack, having a miraculous transformation into *Why not me?* Then, the glorious moment came when *Not me!* and *Why me?* ripped completely off, replaced by *Real me.*

My heavenly Father held me on the dance floor of life during those years of *Not me!* and *Why me?,* but sometimes my feet didn't move with the rhythm so well. That's because He was humming a new and different tune in my ear the whole time, a tune I didn't know. A new tune. He never let me go during those dances of life; instead, He believed I would eventually be dancing to that other tune, the tune of *The Real Life Dance*. He saw possibilities in me that I never saw.

In this dance, I can be honest with myself and with my Father. I don't have to pretend to be a princess because He knows better! He sees my inner thoughts and knows that I'm not always squeaky clean. He hears my cries of frustration and knows that I've got a long way to go in this Christian life. Though I know there could be more times when I might temporarily cry out, "It's not fair! Why me?" I realize that I actually know better. It's taken many years of God's patience to move me into real life, and I wouldn't trade this way of being for anything. I never want to go back.

Every morning when I awake, my Father takes my hand and invites me to a new morning of dancing. He holds me tightly, sways with me to the music of a new dawn, and whispers in my ear.

"You are my darling real life daughter! I am so glad that you see things differently now. You have a view that shows growth, and I like that. I have a secret to tell you. Listen closely. *You are still a princess to me*! Listen closer to this. Even princesses have to walk on the floor like every body else. Even princesses are subject to hazards of nature, sickness of body, and all other calamities common to man. That's because Satan is extra busy with his work.

"Stick with me. Let me hold you on this dance floor, and when those things happen, I'll be right there with you before they even happen. That way, you and I together can move through whatever is thrown your way. I don't plan to go anywhere else. I'm staying right here with you."

I get out of bed, stretch and take my first step onto the dance floor. The floor is real-life cold. I need a real-life wash of my face. My tummy is real-life hungry for breakfast! I sense deep inside that this is where He has wanted me all along. I'm grateful. I'm safe and content. I love this honest relationship that my Father and I now have. I can tell Him anything, the good and the not-so-good. I can cry. I can get upset and angry. I can tell Him exactly how I feel, and He stays with me. Joyfully, I step into His Presence as we begin another day on the dance floor of Real Life.

To My Reader: Have you looked at some of your recent troubles with a *why me*? attitude? Does life seem unfair and you seem to spend more time growling and pouting instead of living life to the fullest? Have you spent good hours angry over the injustices that come with *not me*? Life hands out pain to the good as well as the not-so-good. Becoming real involves your bending your will to His will as He teaches you truths about yourself you have never seen before. I'd like to offer a prayer to help you in finding your real self.

Prayer: Father, I'm sort of afraid of tearing down the walls I live under in order to find the real me. I am not sure how to do it. I don't want to spend the rest of my life pretending, worrying, trying to be someone I am not. Please peel the layers of pride and pretense away and help me to find who I am. In Jesus' Name I pray, Amen.

Chapter Thirteen

Moonlight Dance of Grace

It's evening, and you are walking alone on the beach. The sand feels good beneath your toes, and the water is amazingly calm. The moon gives a glow to the falling darkness as the stars sparkle above. The view is perfect, but you are not. With every step you take and with every minute that passes, you are reminded of who you are and why your heart is heavy. Talking about it is too dangerous. Others would not understand. Telling someone would bring condemnation. It is better to keep your thoughts to yourself, and yet that is why you feel this way. It's all inside. Your mistakes are knotted in your heart like a yarn of dark string. Sometimes you think you will suffocate if you cannot get any relief. But where? How? When?

You are sure no one has ever felt this way before. You wonder about those who have made wrong choices and seemed not to care. They appear to go on unhindered in their role in life. They don't stop to evaluate or review. It seems, at least to you, that they have some sort of secret you've never heard of, a secret that keeps them guilt-free. Maybe you have your guilt and theirs too. Maybe that's how it works. Perhaps you deserve all this guilt. After all, what you have done, were it known, would make others ignore you. You would be the subject at the hair salons, the talk in the neighborhood and the embarrassment of your church. You have it all figured out. Keep quiet. Suffer alone. It's best that way. No one will understand.

You take a few more steps, watching your feet bury into the wet sand and trying to remember a time when you didn't feel this way. Was there such a time? Was there a time when you felt guilt-free, light and carefree? If so, it was years ago. Life has crushed you in more ways than you care to recall. Hard realities have crashed your party of fun. You think back to the times when you could have acted differently, and you didn't, and you want to put a big S on your forehead for STUPID! In your mind, you are sure no one has ever felt this low before or messed up quite this badly.

For some strange reason, women seem to want to become a member of the **Guilty Society**. Some even vote themselves president! Whether imposed by someone else, or because of a poor choice they made, women seem to think that once they get on the Ferris Wheel of guilt, a never-ending, continual guilt cycle covers every new day. Accepting their guilt and blame seems to be the only thing to do.

Acknowledging what they have done by hammering guilt into their souls each day is easier than accepting freedom. Somebody has to pay, and it might as well be them!

So, on you walk, and as the moonlight brushes your hair, you notice something strange near the dunes. Your curiosity wins, and you walk closer. What is this? Large words are written into the sand. They appear deep and bold, and you get the idea that not even a strong wind could blow them away. With just enough light to see, you stop in front of the first word. It reads **For.**

For? What kind of message is that? So you move to the right a bit and see the next word, just as large, just as sure. **all**. **For all**. You glance at the next word. **have**. **For all have**. Who would write such strange words in the sand? You don't want to stop, so you move on another few steps. **sinned. For all have sinned**. Now, you cannot stop. You walk quickly as the next words come into focus.

For all have sinned and fall short of the glory of God!

Great! That's all you need. A condemning beach! A beach that knows your background? What is this!

You start running away from the words, but something pulls you back. More words are written, and these are even bigger. You try not to look, but the words seem confident, drawing you into them. You decide to get it over with quickly. So, you start running past each word, speaking each out loud as you pass by.

For all have sinned and fall short of the glory of God and are justified freely by His GRACE through the redemption that came by Christ Jesus.

Okay. Who out here on the beach knows about your past and wants to preach you a sermon? Sure, you have heard words like *justified, grace, redemption and Jesus Christ*! You've been in church! Who would write them in the sand? Why?

The long run on the beach has made you tired, so you sit down close to that last word, **Jesus.** You are angry. Even if somebody didn't put this in the sand for you, why have you found it? Who is trying to get a message to you? Besides, all you want to do is walk and drink in the beauty of the night. You didn't come here to think about anything.

Time passes. You continue to stay where you are. The ocean seems almost motionless, the waves barely lapping the sand. The moon seems to cast a stronger glow, and suddenly something inside of you accepts the moonlight as part of your healing, but you don't even know why. A feeling of peace comes over you, and you decide to lie back on the sand. Never mind your hair or your clothes. How long has it been since you abandoned yourself to do something like this? You are the one who always remains in control. Life moves easier that way. Don't let anybody in. Make a list of what you will do each day and do it. Don't deviate. Never allow someone else to have the control.

Relaxing into the sand reminds you of when you were a child and your worries could never snuff out your fun. For the first time ever, you begin to think about when fun left you. When did life get so hard? When did you find yourself a captive on this planet? When was your joy removed?

Your life begins to replay as you think of those times when you went against the teachings of your parents, your church, or your own inner values. Those times when you didn't live up to the higher life that you knew was meant for you. Sometimes you were an innocent victim of someone else's control, and the guilt from those times seems as strong as the guilt of your own choices. When did you first drop your innocence into the pit of no return?

If you could just hear something right now, it would really help. The ocean is too still. No sounds of anyone can be heard nearby. Surely your heartbeat can be heard at the closest condo. With each loud beat, you begin to reflect on your life. The reminders don't feel good. Your negative thoughts about other people make you want to scream. What is happening to you? Why is there a sudden drum roll of your past, coming quickly and relentlessly, starting when you were a child? You put your hand over your eyes to try to stop the movie, but nothing will make it stop, so you get up and start to run away. Away from those words.

Those words. That's when all this self- reflection started! If you can just get away from those words in the sand, but they seem to fall over you like a covering, enfolding you, keeping you from running, making you stay. You sit back down and the peace drifts back into you once again.

Suddenly, you know you have to read those words again. A strange compulsion pulls you back to the first word. You <u>need</u> to read them again, so you begin walking slowly as each word rests in your mind.

You understand the first four. **For all have sinned.** Sunday School taught you about that. Nobody is perfect. You've heard that all your life. You realize you are a part of the human race and to think you're perfect would be ludicrous. We all make mistakes. Wait a minute. You've never thought about this before, but what exactly is sin? When you make a mistake, is that a sin? What's the difference?

Like morning dew falling into your heart, you seem to instinctively know. The meaning comes quickly. Sin is claiming my right to myself, thinking that I matter more than anyone else matters, that my rights are more important than those of others. Sin makes me step on anyone to get what I want. Sin causes me to forget others in my attempt to rise higher in my own goals. Sin stops me short of the calling to come higher. I can't go higher when self is on the throne. Sin, therefore, includes mistakes that were consciously chosen in order to exalt Self. Sin is a barrier between God and man. A holy God abhors sin because sin places a barrier between Him and the relationship He craves with us. To God, sin is ugly, dark, and foul. To me, when I am in the sin, I don't see ugly, dark, or foul. I see only that I am getting what I want. For the moment. The guilt comes later.

You sit back and take a deep breath. Where did all of that come from? Now you are curious. What did the next words say? You cannot remember, so you practically trip on your feet to find them.

And fall short of the glory of God. Once again, meaning falls into you, and without knowing how you know, you just know. *For all have sinned and fall short of His radiant beauty, His splendor, His magnificence!*

That makes sense. Who of us can measure up to God? Who of us can be worthy of even coming into His presence? Who of us is good enough to even give Him our worshipful adoration?

You don't know why, but as the tears come, you sit back down. If this be really true, then you are sunk. You've had it. No hope at all is available for you. You of all people cannot measure up. Who is doing this to you? You decide to get up and walk away.

You cannot. You are compelled once again to read the remaining words. You don't want to, but you seem to have no choice. Something greater than you is pulling you.

You move quickly past each one, soaking the words into your heart and looking for understanding. There's got to be more than just the downer of these first words. You feel rotten inside because you know you have sinned and fallen short of the glory of God. Short? Way short. Not even in the same playing field with God. Whoever put these words in the sand knows you too well. You are angry at them and curious too. You continue walking.

And are justified freely by His grace. You can't seem to stop the flow of words now that pour into your consciousness. **Justified** is when all the wrongs in you are made right. *Justify* means that wrongs are forgotten as if they never happened. The slate is wiped clean. Everything is evened up.

That sounds too easy. You mean all that you ever did can just go away, just like that, with the snap of a finger? You've never been one to accept anything that was too easy and were always suspicious of that. All you've ever gotten came through hard work. You don't trust these words. How could they be true? It couldn't happen. Just couldn't.

You can't stop, however, so you continue on. **Freely by His grace.** Whoa. Nothing worth anything has ever been free! Something's wrong here. Freely by whose grace? Surely not God? Would God actually hand you something that is free when your life has been marked by those things that kept you falling short of His glory. It makes no sense!

The meaning of **Grace** sifts into your heart: The overflowing favor of God. God favors you? God favors you with overflowing favor? It never stops? It always flows? What is it that overflows? God's *nature* overflows. His *love* and *forgiveness* overflow. Like the moonlight tonight. The moonlight hasn't stopped. It has continued to flow, even though you knew in your heart that your sins should have gotten you only total darkness. Maybe God's grace is like the moonlight: not so bright that you are overcome with light, but just enough light to get you from step to step. Just enough light for you to read each word as you walk past it.

But how? Why? Why would a holy God in whose presence sinners always fall short, give free grace?

The concluding words give the answer. **Through the redemption that came by Jesus Christ.** What is redemption? The words come slowly and tenderly: *Redemption* means that Jesus made it possible for any and every person to be born into the Kingdom where He lives.

You sit down, realizing that something warm is moving all through you. Something that says to you the incredible, unbelievable news that you, *even you*, are one of those persons who can be born into the Kingdom of Jesus. Through Jesus. Because of Jesus. Only because of Jesus. A smile begins to form on your lips. Is it truly possible that you might be able to actually live free from your past sins? By accepting and realizing what Jesus came to do, can you live inside a second chance? Can it be possible that all you have ever done can be made clean? It is too good to be true. New tears fall, but this time they fall from a wonderful sense of this unbelievable truth.

Wait. Someone is coming. You don't want to see anyone! This is your private time on the beach. Maybe it's the one who wrote the words, and they're coming back to see if the tide has washed them away. Quickly, you try to blot your eyes and get up, but the figure calls to you. Not an audible call, but a sure and clear one just the same.

He moves toward you, reaches for your hand and you feel the most comfort and warmth you have ever felt. You feel no fear. The eyes are too kind. Could it be that this is…no, surely it can't be God!

The most beautiful music you have ever heard fills the beach. He pulls you closer, and everything inside of you relaxes. You feel safer than you ever have felt.

Your Father says, "You are my child. I made you for myself. I want so much for you to understand that all you have ever done can fall under the redemption of My Son. It is grace, through Jesus, that makes our relationship possible. Won't you come now and dance with me?"

Easily you move into the rhythm of His dance. He says nothing, but you know in your heart everything He is thinking just as He knows what you are thinking. The intimacy is beautiful, sweet and cleansing. You never knew it could be like this. For some reason, you only heard the negative sound of judgment all of your life. Maybe you were the one making it all so hard. But, now, it's so different. You don't have to work to get His grace. Jesus gives it to you freely just because that's the way He operates. That's His plan. His divine plan. He came so that sinners like you could be justified for free by His grace, the grace that came when His plan included your becoming a part of His kingdom!

You pull closer to the strong arms of God and hear His heartbeat. With each regular beat, you hear these words: *justified freely; by His grace; through His redemption; it all comes from Jesus Christ.*

Over and over the same words speak a continuous song of love into your spirit as you remain on the sand with your Father. Everything you have ever been ashamed of comes pouring out through your tears as you rest your head on his chest. You confess it all and ask for His forgiveness and grace. As you look up into His eyes and see the compassion of His face, you realize He's known all of this all along. He was just waiting for you to accept His dance.

Grace comes like the moon. It doesn't overpower you. It's just always there. Steady. Loyal. Clear. Lighting the path before you. That's when you realize the name of the dance. It's the Moonlight Dance of Grace. Your Father's grace, freely given to you, will make all the difference in your life.

You look into His eyes and ask the obvious question, the question that will free you from the past and usher you into a new life of grace, "How do I do it?"

He smiles and says, "You don't do it. Jesus has already done it for you. You asked earlier if everything goes away with just the snap of your finger. Actually, it took the snap of a whip on the back of Jesus and the hammer of the nails into his flesh. The gift is simply for you to accept. It's free, and then you and I can have that Father-Daughter relationship that we both want. The next time you sin, come talk with me about it. The same grace will always be waiting to help you get through it. I always give grace. I always forgive."

You understand. You accept His Son. You accept His gift of grace. You feel lighter, younger and so very free. Finally, the morning is dawning and your Father gently lets you go as He walks away.

"No, wait," you say. "Don't leave me. This has been the best night of my life."

"Don't worry," you hear His calm assurance. "I'm always by your side. Just look for me. You'll see. I'm always there."

You want to keep this feeling forever. You never want it to leave you. You feel His words so strongly surging through all of you, like a swiftly moving stream. You hear these words: "Walk with Me each day, and you will always feel My touch. Talk with Me about your faults, your problems. We have a relationship now because you have accepted My Son. You are clean. All things are made new. When life gets difficult, take my hand, lean on my chest, and we'll dance."

You know you can trust Him. Joyfully, you turn around and walk away, but you will never forget the words He wrote for you on the sand: **For all have sinned and fall short of the glory of God and are justified freely by His grace through the redemption that came by Christ Jesus. (Romans 3:23-24)**

It feels so good to have a Father who understands. You will sleep well tonight. Your life will never be the same.

To My Reader: We have trouble accepting a gift that is free, but Paul tells us in this verse in Romans that justification is free. That simply means we are made right. All of our wrongs are made right. That's justification, and it does not cost us anything. Jesus gives that to us as a free gift. What a blessing to know we have a Savior who does not make us pay. Instead, he paid for our redemption with His life. What a gift. What a Savior.

Prayer: Thank you for taking all of my sin, and doing it without cost to me. I don't understand it all, but I willingly agree to accept it all. Thank you for justifying me freely. You fill me like the moonlight, gently, beautifully and just at the right time. In Jesus' Name, Amen.

Chapter Fourteen

Dance of The Lamb

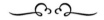

Your Father God takes your hand. Without any explanation, He guides you once more to the Dance Floor of Life. He has a lamb under one arm. It's a bit tough to dance with Him like this. The legs of the lamb are tied together. If he gets away, he can't run anywhere. It seems so senseless, so cruel. You are curious. Wonder why his legs are tied, and why in the world does God want to bring a lamb to the dance floor?

As the music begins, your Father starts telling a story. Each scene appears as a vivid drawing on a canvas beside you. The first drawing is of a beautiful garden.

"I made this garden for my first children. I wanted to give them the best of everything. Nothing was too good for them. Around them I placed sweet-smelling trees and plants, each bursting forth with brilliant color. I gave them streams to bathe in and fruit to eat.

"Remember that I have talked to you before about that one tree that I forbade them to eat: The Tree of the Knowledge of Good and Evil. I told them if they did, they would surely die. Not *maybe* die. Not *possibly*, but surely. They were too curious about that one tree. You may remember from previous dances that I told you how Satan came to Eve in the form of a crawling snake, enticing her to try the fruit of that tree. His argument was compelling, because Eve took a piece. Then she went to Adam and offered some to him. He ate it.

"It only took one bite, but with that one bite, everything in the garden changed. Every animal and plant took on death, and My prized creation, man and woman, took on sin and death. No longer would there be luscious fruit trees that perpetually reproduced good fruit. Trees and plants, as well as animals would eventually die. Mankind would now know about sin and have the nature that would cause them to sin and to die.

"As soon as sin entered the world through the disobedience of Adam and Eve, My love entered the world even stronger. Sin could not wipe out My love. Sin could never make Me give up on my children. Adam and Eve hid from Me because they were ashamed of their nakedness. Before they ate the forbidden fruit, they were naked and unashamed, but now they felt shame. I wanted to show them that nothing they could ever do would make me change my mind about them. I made them in love. I would walk with them through their blunders, loving them just as much. I was disappointed in their disobedience, but being disappointed is not the same as not loving. I don't stay inside disappointments. I only stay inside love.

"I had to show them how my love continues, no matter that they disobeyed. I did that through teaching them about forgiveness. They had to learn that they could repent, and I would forgive. I wanted my children to learn that I never turn my back on them. I had to show them that even though I was upset over their disobedience, my love for them remained. I decided to cover the shame of their nakedness.

"I sewed an outfit for each of them from the skin of an animal. Blood was shed as I brought about the very first sacrifice. As the blood fell, I called My Son Jesus to My side. I told My Son that I wanted Him to watch what I was doing with this animal. I told Him that this was a picture of what He would do later. I told Him to *watch the blood fall* as I cut the animal's skin. He understood."

The second drawing appears on the canvas. It is an artist's picture of Adam and Eve in the clothes their Father sewed for them. (Genesis 3:21)

"I had a plan in mind, and many years after Adam and Eve, my servant Abraham was told to kill his only son, Isaac. He obediently followed my instructions. He took Isaac to an altar and tied him down. He drew his sharp instrument, ready to do what was going to break his heart, but I never intended for him to kill the child of the promise. Isaac had a great purpose, and he would become a strong leader. I had to see if Abraham would obey.

"When Abraham obeyed, I stopped Him just as he was going to put the knife through Isaac. Just in time, I sent a ram into the thick brush. Abraham heard something moving, and he caught the lamb. The lamb became the sacrifice. (Genesis 22:13) As the lamb was slain, I called My Son Jesus to My side. *'Watch the blood fall.'* He understood."

A third picture appears, and in large view, you see a lamb being substituted for Isaac. The lamb was slain so that Isaac could go free.

"My children grew in numbers and became slaves of a cruel pharaoh. They lived in Egypt, but I wanted them in Canaan, the land I promised them. I chose Moses to bring them out of Egypt. Pharaoh fought every idea Moses presented. He was determined to keep my children in slavery.

"I wanted to set my people free, so I gave instructions to Moses. He was to tell each man to slaughter a lamb for his household. Each family was to take some of the lamb's blood and put it on the sides and tops of their doorframes. Every Israelite home was to do this. Then, I went through the land, striking down each first-born Egyptian child, but because of the blood on the doorposts of my children, I passed over their homes. (Exodus 12:12-13)

"As this happened, I called my Son Jesus over to my side. *'Watch the blood fall* as each lamb is slain.' He watched, and He understood.

"I showed Jesus the blood smeared on each door-post. I explained that the blood protected that home from danger. He understood that too."

You watch as another canvas appears, this one showing thousands of lambs being killed for the protection of the Israelites' homes. The picture is gruesome. Jesus might have understood. But, you don't.

Your Father continues. "Later, I taught this plan to my servant Moses, and he was to teach my Hebrew children. I taught him that forgiveness comes through the shedding of blood. There would never be any other way. Blood brings forgiveness. In the book of Leviticus I made this clear when I said to Moses, *For the life of a creature is in the blood, and I have given it to you to make atonement for yourselves on the altar; it is the blood that makes atonement for one's life.'* (Leviticus 17:11)

"So, the people brought their sins to the priest who represented Me. The priest would then kill an animal, take its blood and sprinkle it on the altar for atonement for sin. When I first showed this to Moses, I called My Son Jesus over to My side. (Leviticus 16:18) *'Watch the blood fall,'* I said to My Son. He understood.

"My Hebrew people did this for years and years. They could not see my Son nearby, but all through those years, He watched as each animal was slain according to my directions. He stood especially close by when a lamb was slain. *He saw the blood fall.* He understood."

But, *you* still don't understand. "Why blood? Why the killing of innocent animals? Why? Isn't there any other way?"

Your Father is silent as He moves you around the dance floor. On all sides of the Dance Floor, bright lights shine. On every wall, from top to bottom, a huge picture of a slain lamb appears. You decide you're ready to go home. You don't like all this blood. Too many lambs. Too much blood. You can almost hear the lambs crying as their lives are taken away from them. And they are innocent! They don't deserve this!

Your Father knows what you are thinking. "Do you have a better plan to forgive sin?"

"Not really," you answer. "But, if you'll give me some time, I'm sure I can come up with something that is not quite so gory!"

"Life has to be given by one in order for life to be received by another" your Father quietly responds. "Something has to die in order for something else to live. A sacrifice has to happen. When you eat meat for nourishment, an animal's life is taken first. It is the same in the spiritual realm. Something dies so that others may live."

Another picture appears. John the Baptist stands in the water baptizing. Jesus comes towards him, and John says in a loud voice, "Look, the Lamb of God, who takes away the sin of the world." (John 1:29)

You have been watching lambs all through this dance. Why is John calling Jesus the Lamb who takes away the sin of the world?

Another picture appears. It is Jesus on the cross. There are words written all over him. Terrible words. Words that don't belong on Jesus. You look closer. Each word appears in bold letters. **Unkindness, gossip, murder, slander, disloyalty, cheating, grudges, coveting, lying, hate, dishonesty, failures, diseases, fear**. The list goes on and on. There is not one place on the body of Jesus without a word.

Wait. Something is happening. Something is falling on your clothes. Quickly you realize it is blood, and you look at the lamb your Father is holding. The blood is coming from the lamb. You don't understand, but soon the blood covers all your clothes. Then, quietly and without fuss, the lamb dies.

At that moment, into the silence of the Dance Floor comes a scream louder than any you have ever heard before. It's Jesus! The scream is one of intense pain. Your Father looks lovingly at His Son on the cross. His eyes are sad. Then, your Father God does a strange thing. He turns away from Jesus. He turns away from His Son! He begins to move our dance to the other side of the room. Why doesn't He run to help His Son. He could do it. He could take Jesus off of the cross. Yet, He continues to turn the other way.

Your body tenses as you move closer to your Father. He holds you tightly as the two of you continue the dance. Soon, a tear falls from His face onto your cheek.

The scream stops. The Lamb dies. The Father cries. The final sacrifice is given.

You are quiet for what seems like hours. You can only hear the loud, steady beating of your Father's heart and the clear sound of His love. You are amazed that when His Son is dying, He is holding you instead of hurrying to Jesus. It's like somehow you are the main focus of God during the death of the Lamb.

"You are," His voice whispers.

Another picture appears. The Lamb that had been slain was now alive and standing. You are now surrounded by the sound of angels flapping their wings as the praises of others form a melodious offer of praise.

"Worthy is the Lamb," you hear over and over again. Louder and louder it gets. "Worthy is the Lamb!"

Your Father begins to move around the floor with new energy. The chorus continues until you join in, the words coming automatically into your consciousness as if you had memorized them.

"Worthy is the Lamb, who was slain, to receive power and wealth and wisdom and strength and honor and glory and praise!" (Revelation 5:12)

Somehow, it is as if a new and brighter intelligence is explaining everything to you. Now, you understand. Now, it all makes sense.

Jesus is the Lamb of God. He came to earth to die. When his blood fell, the final sacrifice for sin was given. All that went on before Jesus was the preamble. It was the substitute for forgiveness until the real substitute came along. Jesus took your sin. Death and sin no longer hold you in their deadening grip. You can still sin, but it's not because you have to. *You don't have to*. You don't have to let anything enslave you to its habit, its temptation or its control.

The power of sin's control has been broken through the blood of Jesus, the Lamb of God. Just like the houses that were passed over in Egypt because of the blood of a lamb, so the power of sin and death passes over you because of the blood of the Lamb, Jesus.

You are still in the world, so temptation remains. But, you are free to say NO. Death holds no fear. Your sins are gone. Just at the lamb was slain in Isaac's place, The Lamb of God is now slain so that you can go free.

You can stand no longer. Instead, you fall down and bow before Him.

This is the message of the Dance of the Lamb.

To My Reader: The Dance of the Lamb is compelling and much better than any thing you or I could ever plan. Throughout history, Jesus watched the lambs. Then, He moved to earth and became the Lamb. There will never be a need for any other sacrifice, but sometimes we have great difficulty grasping this concept. It is best if you accept it, understand what you can of it, and then ask God to enlighten your spirit further. The main thing I hope you can do after this Dance is to begin to understand the connection between the blood of Jesus and the forgiveness of your sin. Without the shedding of Jesus' blood, there is no forgiveness of sin. What a plan! What a Savior! Amen!

Prayer Dear Jesus, I confess to not completely understanding this. But, it is our Father's plan, not mine. So, I want to hear this message. I want to accept that what you did for me on the cross settles the question of my guilt forever. You took my guilt and shame upon your body, went to the cross and became the sacrifice God required. It should have been me up there. I should have died for my own shame, but that's not God's way. You covered Adam and Eve, and now you cover me. Thank you for this Dance. Hold me closely as I seek to understand this better and to receive its message completely. In the Lamb's Name I pray, Amen.

Chapter Fifteen

Dancing at the Laundromat

Dancing the love dance is captivating, exciting and fun. We like the thought of being loved unconditionally by a heavenly Father who has our best interest at heart. Walking on the dance floor of life with our Father might not come naturally at first, but we can trust this dance. We can trust the arms we cling to as we hesitantly move toward the center of the dance floor.

However, we cannot be complete with only a love dance. As God's love becomes a reality in our lives, another dance exists that we are compelled to learn. This dance comes because of the kindness of the One who holds us through the days of our dance. When we recognize His heart of mercy toward us, we realize who we really are. Past sins rise to haunt us. Present mistakes carry a rank odor not noticed before. Suddenly, those errors we have buried under the dirt of our pride seem to scream in our ears. We recognize that we aren't pure. We aren't innocent. We become obsessed with the prison we live in, realizing that we cannot escape the past or control the future.

Before this time, we swept our faults into the basement of our lives. Now, however, these same faults have filled the entire basement and are oozing up the stairs, rising dangerously close to our comfort zone. Our sinful, stubborn, rebellious nature needs a complete overhaul. Conviction sets in. We are sincerely sorry for hurting others. We would give anything if we had not made that certain decision. We feel that we are no longer any good. We are broken in heart, remorseful in spirit, and hopeless for anything better. In short, we are miserable.

We look down at our clothes. They may carry brand names, but they don't look that good to us now. All we see are filthy rags. Consumed with guilt, we recognize that our sinful stains must be placed in the laundry where they will get a complete overall. Somewhere in the midst of our self-examination comes, however, the frightening knowledge that we don't have the right kind of money to operate the washing machine! We look around the laundromat, searching for detergent and bleach. None exists. All we can do is place our dirty laundry in the washing machine, but we cannot turn it on! We cannot add detergent. We cannot bleach the worst spots. We can't do anything about the dirt of our lives. We are helpless to make ourselves clean.

Being accustomed to paying for what we obtain in this world, we suppose now that we can do nothing more. We have made our own hell on earth, and finding peace for our sordid sins seems impossible.

Death would be better than living with so many regrets! You ask God if you can die. That's exactly what He's been waiting to hear.

He's not thinking of our final death. That death will happen only once. This death is a death of our own choosing. Daily deaths. Many deaths, which take place as we recognize we have a higher calling than living in the basement. It is a death in which we willingly participate so that we might achieve a loftier goal. We decide to die to self-interests that interfere with God's touch on our lives. We decide to die to self-exaltation, in order to exalt Him. We decide to die to selfishness, rebellion, and acceptance of sin's pulls. We die to our lower nature being in control. We die to any perversion we carry in our hearts and any willful acts of wrongdoing in which we are actively involved. We die to unhealthy thought patterns and stubbornness. We choose to die to having our own way about things and to self-absorption. We die to our need to control, to be noticed, to be first. We lay all of this on the altar, giving God permission to continue to show us areas that need to die.

So, here you are, standing alone in the laundromat, wearing your stained rags and stained heart and not knowing how in the world you can make things better. That's when God walks in. Others are there, but no one else seems to notice Him. His divine appointment is just for you. In one instant, you realize that God has Someone with Him, and then, in some mysterious yet marvelous way, Jesus appears in the very same spot God stood. You hear Jesus but not audibly. You hear him with the ears of your spirit as He lets you know how to get the washing machine started.

"I am the way," He says to your spirit. Instinctively you know that Jesus is referring to your cleansing. "I am the Way," He repeats, and immediately you know that everything inside of you yearns for what Jesus has to offer. "Turn it all over to me," He says. "Give up all that keeps you in prison. Repent, and I will wash your stains of sin away."

You expected that it would be harder than this. You reach in your pocket and pull out the pocket linings to show Jesus that you have no money. You have nothing at all to give Him for this cleansing. You have done nothing to obtain a right to anything pertaining to Jesus. It just can't be this easy. Isn't there more you must do?

Because you've been so adept at being in control, you tell Him a list of things you'll be glad to do in return for this cleansing. You offer to feed the hungry and give clothes to those who are cold. You'd be so happy to volunteer at the soup kitchen once a week and help repair broken bicycles next Christmas. Jesus only listens.

He says again, "I am the Way. Volunteer work is not the Way. Feeding and clothing others is not the Way. Those things are good, but *I am the Way*. Nothing else substitutes for Me." Jesus is firm. "Those who try to turn human resources or commitments into the Way will end up still in prison. You cannot pay for My services. What I give is free."

Sadly, you leave the laundromat feeling hopeless. "Nothing is free," you repeat to yourself over and over until you finally sit down on a nearby bench, watching the birds discover bits of food underneath the covering of fallen leaves. You look up at the empty branches, thinking of the new growth that will come after the winter's freeze.

You hear a voice. He is calling you to dance. At first you decline, feeling so completely unworthy to even be near this One who gives free gifts. You mark yourself unworthy, knowing you have no right to receive anything. He calls again, and slowly you move His way, a strange compulsion luring you on.

Once you reach Him you can't help but be drawn to His magnetic personality, His all-consuming love! Eagerly, you fall into His embrace.

Your Father points to that same tree, and says gently, "Look. The tree doesn't suffer when the leaves fall and die. Before it falls to the ground, each dead leaf places the kiss of life in its spot on the limb. Fresh, green leaves are born when the time is right. This new life doesn't cost the tree anything, but turning down new life would cause the tree everything. The tree, in refusing spring's favor, would always remain barren, living beneath the reason it was made. Trees are made to produce new life. So are you."

Somehow, without your knowing how, Jesus now becomes your Partner. You look into His eyes of love, resting your confusion against the contentment of being in His embrace. You want to repent. You know you need to, but you still struggle with

His handing you a free gift in exchange for the mess you've made of your life.

He speaks, the words of His melody moving through your soul. "If you want to live with me, not only now but forever, repentance is necessary. No longer can it be your way. I am the Way."

You have to ask. You must ask. "Why can't I live with you forever just because you love me? Isn't that enough?"

He answered. "Love gave. Now, you must receive. That's the only way that you can have the best Love has to offer. Receive it all, not just the feelings of acceptance without conditions. Receive everything the Father planned. He planned for your future based on my death. I died, and then I came back! Love keeps you always before Our face. Love never stops. Love never gives up on you. Still, you must repent of who you are, your shortcomings and your sins, and allow me to touch each weakness with my healing power. Freedom only comes in one way. You must receive by repenting and by dying to the self in you, that self who wants to be the main actor on life's stage."

You are thoughtful. "That doesn't sound like much fun!"

Jesus answered your thoughts. "You think prison is more fun?"

It seems that the two of you dance for a long, long time. Jesus is patient as you remain silent. As you dance, you think of that tree as an instant replay of events quickly moves through your mind. If each fallen leaf places the kiss of life at its vacant spot, thus giving birth to a new green leaf, then maybe the same could happen with you. You understand that as you repent of each negative in your life and purposely choose death to self, then maybe each death, when handed to Jesus, produces new birth in that very same spot! Only with His touch and His forgiveness could this be possible. Just as old leaves fall to the ground, your chains could also fall to the ground. In place of death, new life would come into every area given over to Love. It was beginning to make sense. Repentance means turning completely around from where you were and going the other way, letting go of the past through the power of forgiveness and moving toward new life in Jesus.

Jesus starts, "I can tell you still struggle with My gift being free. Just trust Me on this one."

Now you are seeing in your mind the scene from the laundromat. "You would really put my sins through the wash? All the dirt would be gone? You'd do that for me?"

He smiles. "I already did. Love took care of it on the cross. You must now accept what Love did, but let's move back to the laundromat."

You follow Him there. He says, "It isn't water that washes you clean. My laundromat has my blood in the washing machines. My blood is the only thing that can make you clean. My blood makes your filthy rags white. It is My blood that cleanses you. My blood had to be shed in order for you to be free.

"Don't try to figure it all out. Just accept it. Receive what I did. God required blood. You don't have to understand why. You just must accept that

I became submissive to what our Father wanted me to do. It was His plan. It still is His plan for each person."

As Jesus takes your hand, you close your eyes, continuing to sway with the music as the two of you dance in the laundromat. You are beginning to realize that this dance is the only one that makes you free enough to trust this gift of God. Free to let go! Free to be alive! Free to go before the face of God unhampered, knowing that forgiveness is available always, even for you! Alive enough to understand that Jesus hates your chains so much that He died to saw those chains in two!

You thought that freedom was for someone else or that you would be bound forever to your poor choices. You felt to admit mistakes was to indicate a weakness. Understanding that to admit mistakes and sins shows growth instead means you have to switch gears completely in your thinking. Thoughtfully, you take your hand out of His. You kneel right there at the laundromat, on the dance floor of your life. Somehow you know that everything has been leading you to this point. You look into His eyes.

"Jesus, will You help me? I repent of every thought I've ever had that was wrong and every decision that has hurt You. I die to all that is contrary to Your desires for me. Like fallen leaves, I want to throw off my self-sufficiency, giving birth to Your-sufficiency in its place. When the old tries to slip into self-sufficiency, I will bow once more, repent, and die to whatever is trying to pull me down. With Your help, I know I can do this. Amen."

Chains drop. Heaven opens. Freedom comes. It's all yours when you understand how to do it. You are glad you let go. Glad to be free. The God of Release releases you! Gone are past and present mistakes! Gone forever! The blackboard of your life is erased completely!

No sense in even bringing those sins up before the Lord again. It's taken care of. It's over. Just like the barren tree, you are, through repentance, born anew. A new shoot is coming forth. Dazzling with its color! Glorious in its freedom!

What is that you now hear? Not only the music of the Repentance Dance, but also something more. Voices singing! Hands clapping! Heavenly music! You feel wonderful! Light and free! Relaxed! Unbelievably content! You are amazed!

It's angels. They're making a fuss over *you*. You thought claps for you ended when you sang a solo in the kindergarten choir.

"I tell you that in the same way there will be more rejoicing in heaven over one sinner who repents than over ninety-nine righteous persons who do not need to repent."(Luke 15:7) Hallelujah! Amen!

To My Reader: Repentance has to come before new birth can begin. What is holding you back from giving all of your mistakes to Jesus? He wants to take them from you. He wants to help you begin new life in Him. You can be free from those chains. You do not have to live under a load of guilt. I'd like to offer a prayer to help you, just in case you're not sure how to begin.

Prayer: Dear Father, I am tired of my old life. I am desperate to start over, to be made new. Will you please help me? I repent of all the sin in my life. I want to name specifically _____. I want to turn around from all my old ways and start fresh with you. Thank you for shedding your blood for my sins. Thank you for dying for me. I want to be completely yours. In your Son's Name, Amen."

Chapter Sixteen

Dancing on the Emmaus Road

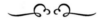

Anew day begins. The sun is making its bright entrance, sweeping away the dark shadows of night. You wish the sun could do that for you and sweep away your downcast mood. Something is disturbing you. A mood is in the air, a mood that is almost chilling. A negative cloud rests over this dance.

Maybe it's because the dance floor is different. It's a long dirt road. Your Father God takes your hand and moves you back two thousand years. You are near a town called Emmaus, seven miles away from Jerusalem. Your Father is very quiet. You suppose you will just stay in the dance and see where He is taking you.

Quickly you recognize that you are not alone on this road. Two men are walking close by. You can hear them talking. Your Father God listens too.

Their conversation carries the dark cloud of discouragement. Jesus has been killed, but these two disciples, one unnamed and the other named Cleopas, do not comprehend. They are disappointed because their dreams and plans for Jesus have been interrupted by His crucifixion. They counted on Him to bring Israel out from underneath the tyranny of the Roman Empire. That dream never happened. Instead, they have a crucified Christ. He was their only hope for salvation from oppression. All those hopes are now gone and in their place is oppression and fear. If indeed Jesus were the Messiah, He is a disappointment to these two men. That is obvious.

They continue their conversation as you and your Father dance nearby. The word on the street is that Jesus has arisen. Some of the women saw Him and told these men and others about this miraculous event. Their questions remained. Rome would always be Rome whether there was a resurrection or not. Persecution would continue. What would a risen Messiah do for Israel that he had not done when He was alive? Even though they had been followers of Jesus, they now felt hopeless and betrayed.

Suddenly, a third person comes alongside these two and asks them what they are talking about. The two men stop in stunned silence, and Cleopas asks this man,

"Are you only a visitor to Jerusalem and do not know the things that have happened there in these few days?" (Luke 24:18)

Their guest on the road questions, "What things?" (Luke 24:19)

They continue walking in their downcast mood, explaining all they know about Jesus who had been crucified. They describe Jesus as a powerful prophet, but that isn't good enough for these two. They had hoped that He would be a military and political influence in the freeing of Israel from Roman rule. That did not happen. Their disappointment is felt as each word drops from their lips.

Just today they heard reports that Jesus had arisen from the dead, but they aren't sure the reports are true. They could be just rumors; besides, the news came from women who saw the empty tomb. Both men comment on how hysterical women can get. However, some of the disciples went to the tomb after the women, and they too saw the empty tomb. After that, the story became believable.

You find yourself cringing, and everything in you tightens. Your Father strokes your head and whispers into your ear, "It's okay. You are dancing in a different period now. You are joining the first eyewitnesses to the resurrection of My Son. Women did not have the status they have now in your era. Don't worry. I made sure that women came into recognition when My Son was on this earth. He valued them and gave them status they had never known before. He traveled with them, taught them, laughed with them and loved them. He tore through the traditions of men by showing that women were of mighty value in our Kingdom. Everything changed for women when My Son walked on earth."

The stranger speaks to the two men. "You are very foolish indeed. You are so slow to believe. All throughout history, the prophets have spoken about the Christ. Did you not understand? Did you not believe? Do you not understand that Christ had to suffer all these things in order to enter his glory?"

The two are silent as the stranger continues. He amazes them with his knowledge of prophecy, quoting verbatim words of old to support His statements. Words come in rapid succession. Starting with history's beginning, this stranger quotes familiar passages, all relating to the Christ: "Soon after Adam and Eve disobeyed, God spoke to the deceiver, Satan, and said of Christ, 'He will crush your head, and you will strike his heel.' (Genesis 3:15) That means that Satan, the Enemy, will repeatedly attempt to defeat Christ during His life on earth, but Christ will ultimately crush Satan's head and win the battle. This was the first introduction of God's plan to defeat Satan and offer salvation to the world through His Son, Jesus Christ."

Familiar verses run through your mind as the stranger gives the prophecy from the Old Testament. With heightened intelligence surpassing anything you have experienced before but that you have known in other dances with your Father, you recall each fulfillment from the New Testament of the promised Messiah.

Psalm 2:7 "The Messiah will be God's Son," is fulfilled in Hebrews 1:5-6.

Psalm 16:8-10 "He will rise from the dead," is fulfilled in Luke 24:5-7.

Psalm 22:1-21 "He will experience agony on the cross," is fulfilled in Matthew 26-27.

Psalm 22:18 "Evil men cast lots for his clothing," is fulfilled in Matthew 27:35.

Psalm 22:15 "He thirsts while on the cross," is fulfilled in John 19:28.

Psalm 22:22 "He will declare God's name," is fulfilled in Hebrews 2:12.

Psalm 34:20 "His bones would not be broken," is fulfilled in John 19:36- 37.

Psalm 40:6-8 "He came to do God's will," is fulfilled in Hebrews 10:5-7.

Psalm 41:9, "His close friend will betray Him," is fulfilled in Luke 22:48.

Psalm 69:21, "He was offered vinegar for his thirst," is fulfilled in Matthew 27:48.

(Passages from *Life Application Study Bible*, New International Version, Zondervan, 1991, pp. 923)

After the Psalms, this stranger moves on to other Prophecies. Amazingly, you know them all. The two disciples are intrigued with this man's knowledge. On and on he moves, once again with unbelievable wisdom.

From portions of Isaiah 53, he adds, "He had no beauty or majesty to attract us to Him, nothing in His appearance that we should desire Him. He was despised and rejected by men, a man of sorrows, and familiar with suffering. Like one from whom men hide their faces, He was despised, and we esteemed Him not. Surely He took up our infirmities and carried our sorrows, yet we considered Him stricken by God, smitten by Him and afflicted. But He was pierced for our transgressions. He was crushed for our iniquities. The punishment that brought us peace was upon Him, and by His wounds, we are healed. He was oppressed and afflicted; yet He did not open His mouth. He was led like a lamb to the slaughter, and as a sheep before his shearers is silent, so He did not open His mouth. He was assigned a grave with the wicked, and with the rich in His death, though He had done no violence, nor was any deceit in His mouth. Yet it was the Lord's will to crush Him and cause Him to suffer, and though the Lord makes His life a guilt offering, He will see His offspring and prolong His days, and the will of the Lord will prosper in His hand. After the suffering of His soul, He will see the light of life, and be satisfied; by His knowledge My righteous servant will justify many, and He will bear their iniquities."

From Zechariah 9 verse 9: "Rejoice greatly, O Daughter of Zion! Shout, Daughter of Jerusalem! See your king comes to you, righteous and having salvation, gentle and riding on a colt, the foal of a donkey."

From Malachi 3:1: "See, I will send my messenger, who will prepare the way before Me. Then suddenly, the Lord you are seeking will come to His temple; the messenger of the covenant, whom you desire, will come," says the Lord Almighty. (The messenger is thought to be John the Baptist who prepared the way for Jesus to come.)

Your heart thrills within you with an excitement you have never known before. Who is this stranger on the Road to Emmaus? Why did your heart leap when He spoke of the prophecies? Why did your spirit surge within you when you realized that Jesus had fulfilled these prophecies?

The day is almost over, and the two disciples are ready to head to their home. The stranger continues on the dirt road until the two urge Him to go home with them. "Stay with us, for it is nearly evening." (Luke 24:29) So, He does.

You begin leading your Father now. "We have to go to their home, too," you say. "I want to hear more. I want to know who this man is who knows so much."

As you and your Father enter the home, you see the three sitting down to eat. It is an ordinary room with a plain kitchen table and wooden benches. No pictures are on the walls and no tablecloth is present. You are puzzled. "Where is the woman of the house? Why hasn't she set a proper table? Why aren't there curtains on the windows and flowers on the table? Instead, on the table is ordinary bread and wine. You ask your Father if you can stop dancing and watch for a while. He agrees. You both move closer to the table.

"When He was at the table with them, He took bread, gave thanks, broke it, and began to give it to them. Then their eyes were opened and they recognized Him, and He disappeared from their sight. They asked each other, 'Were not our hearts burning within us while he talked with us on the road and opened the Scriptures to us?'" (Luke 24:30-32)

Suddenly, the room becomes brighter. The men sit up and look at each other in amazement. *This was Jesus*! They had actually been walking on the

Emmaus Road with Jesus Himself! They did not know! They did not recognize Him. In the breaking of the bread, their eyes were opened to Him in a way they never saw before. They *saw Jesus* when He broke the bread! Amazing!

Quickly, your mind flashes back to the last meal Jesus had with His disciples. "And He took bread, gave thanks and broke it, and gave it to them, saying, 'This is My body given for you; do this in remembrance of Me.'

"In the same way, after supper He took the cup, saying, 'This cup is the new covenant in My blood, which is poured out for you.'" (Luke 22:19-20)

Exciting thoughts move around your spirit. These two disciples have just participated in the first remembrance of Jesus after His death and resurrection. They probably don't have a clue what this means, but just as Jesus said for us to *remember Him* when we take the cup and break the bread, He also intends for us to *see Him* when we participate in this Sacrament. Holy Communion is the time when our hearts put self aside and look for Christ. The men on the road to Emmaus could not see Him until the bread was broken and the wine offered. Likewise, for us, we can find His Presence through Holy Communion. If we prepare our hearts to receive, He will not disappoint us.

You look at your Father as the two men continue starring at one another, wide-eyed over what has just occurred. "How, Father? How do I prepare myself for Holy Communion?"

He answers. "Think back to when my Son first joined the two on the Road to Emmaus. They were self-centered, disappointed and pessimistic. How could they see Him when self ruled? They were focused on their own worries; therefore, they did not recognize my Son. Today, people do the very same thing. While worrying over what did not happen, they almost miss what does happen. These two men almost missed Jesus because their focus was in the wrong place. One way to prepare yourself for Holy Communion is to put your eyes in the right place: on Jesus alone.

"These disciples understand the prophecies, but they fail to realize that Christ's suffering is His path to glory. They are disappointed because I did not rescue My Son from the cross. I could not. He came for this purpose. He came to die. He had to die."

"Well," you ask, "why couldn't they just be thankful that He died for them?"

"Because, before He broke bread, they didn't understand. They wanted a redeemer from Rome. They did not understand Christ came to redeem them from slavery to sin. They did not realize that the death of Jesus and His resurrection brought to them their greatest hope of all."

"Then," you respond, "they should have been grateful, instead of grumbling."

"Make a note of this," My Father answered. "A suffering servant is never popular. People would rather see a conquering hero, riding into Jerusalem on a white horse while carrying a sword in each hand. They want action and excitement. That's not my way."

"How else, Father? How else can I prepare my heart for Holy Communion?"

He stood and took my hand. "Let's finish this dance. I think you'll know more after that."

You dance around the table that holds the broken bread and wine. The two disciples, changed completely by the encounter with Jesus, get up and start running to Jerusalem to share with the eleven original disciples that truly the Lord has arisen. The room, still glowing from the presence of Christ, holds you captive. You and your Father dance around and around the table, while you keep your eyes on the broken bread and wine.

Your Father speaks. "You asked how you could prepare your heart for Holy Communion? You can do that by recognizing its value, and that my Son calls His children to celebrate His life, death and resurrection each time you receive. Take the elements with a thankful heart. Receive as if it is handed to you each time by Jesus Himself. Prepare your heart to commune with My Son as you receive. Repent. Clear out of your heart any unforgiveness, any malice, and any negative feelings you have about others. Come to the Table to eat with My Son and let His love heal you."

You begin to cry. The realization of what Jesus is calling you to do is overwhelming. You don't deserve to come to His Table.

"I know you feel like that. He invites you anyway. He prepares this Table for you, and He welcomes you.

If you stay away, one of His chairs will be empty. He intends for every chair at His Table to be filled with hungry children."

This plain room has now become the most beautiful room you've even seen. There still are no flowers or curtains, but it does not matter. It is beautiful because of the glow left from Jesus, the Light of the World. Your Father drops your hand, takes up the bread and offers you a piece. You hold out your hands to receive. Then, He offers the cup. It is a holy moment for a holy mystery and though you cannot comprehend its meaning, you welcome its usefulness in your life. Never again will you take Communion at your church in the same way. Never again will you walk to the front of the church and have your mind on something else. Your eyes, too, are now open and you have seen the risen Lord.

You stand on holy ground. You will stand on holy ground every time you take Communion. Your Father looks down at you. You look up and smile. You are so glad you agreed to go on this dance. You, like the disciples, were distraught over problems in your life. You, like them, could not see Jesus until He broke the bread representing His body. Hallelujah for the broken body of Christ!

Hallelujah for the remembrance!
Hallelujah for the Table!
Hallelujah for the Redeemer!
Hallelujah that He opens our eyes!

To My Reader: Have you ever been to Emmaus? The invitation is for you. Walk the dusty road with the two disciples. Listen to Jesus quote prophecy. Have your eyes opened as He breaks the bread and extends the cup. You will never be the same. There's something about *opening our eyes* that changes us forever. The road to Emmaus offers that possibility for you. Dance on it today. Find the risen Christ. Embrace Him. Watch Him totally change your life.

Prayer: Jesus, open my eyes so that I can see your glory, your honor, your power and your might. Open my eyes to truly see you as I walk on the Emmaus Road. I'm ready. I want all of you that I can get. Take me to the Communion Table with you and touch me there. I want to see you. In the Name of the Blessed Bread Breaker, Amen.

Chapter Seventeen

Desert Dance

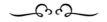

The loneliness of life sometimes falls on you with excessive pain. You have walked this way for so long that you can't imagine life any other way. No one else, or certainly very few, know of your longings, the hurts you have suffered, the pain you carry. Long ago, you forgot about living life. If you can just keep your head above water, keep some of the pressure away, you can survive one more day. You are now an expert at pretending, at moving on, at doing life so you can get from one day to the next.

Loneliness can live with you whether you are in a crowd of people or sitting by yourself in your home. Loneliness rips away at your love for life, your belief in yourself. You want to be involved in life. You want others to invite you to their party; yet each day brings that same pain that shouts in your ear that you are not welcomed, you are not appreciated, you are not valuable.

You make your own rubber stamp and dip it in ink. You plaster its message on your forehead. It reads, "Made To Be Lonely," and each day you live out your self- proclaimed prophecy. It doesn't matter that you have people around you at work or at home. They cannot fill that lonely spot, that hole in your heart. Your pets may jump up and comfort you for a period, but then the loneliness returns. You may walk in a neighborhood overflowing with family life, but you cannot seem to embrace what they have. Instead, you have come to accept your days as being Desert Days. Loneliness carries you to the desert, and loneliness entraps you there. There are no visible prison walls, yet you see them every day.

When you were a little girl, loneliness didn't have much of an entrance into your life. Seasons came when despair sent out its tentacles and pulled you to its uncomfortable side. You learned to live inside the land of make-believe, where baby dolls and pretend games kept you in a world of your own. It was safer there, and you felt comfort. As you grew older, so did the make-believe games. Finally, your pretend world became buried under reality. No secret escaped into a world where colorful images covered all the hurt. One day, loneliness pushed all of those pretend games aside and came to live on your door-steps permanently.

Is there an answer? Is there is a way to fill that void in your life? You probably think it must involve filling the loneliness with shopping, food, things and more projects. You might feel that loneliness can be alleviated only by placing more stuff in your life, more committee work, more community work, even more church work, but at the end of the day, loneliness stays. What is the answer to your need?

Remember when God created you? Do your remember how He put little pink bows everywhere and smiled and giggled because of you? Do you remember how He has held you to His heart so many times, trying to show you His Dance of Love? He is committed into *loving you into knowing Him*. It's a lifetime commitment. He plans to stay.

Loneliness comes when we put expectations on certain people or on circumstances, and then those people or those circumstances don't comply with our needs. We sometimes believe that, if this person or that person would just talk to us or include us in their social functions, we would not experience loneliness any more. If we could just be noticed, just be included, life would take on new meaning. We make it a "dependent on the other person" attitude. When that person gets too busy doing other things, ignores us or doesn't meet our needs, we feel betrayed, and our feeling of loneliness is intensified. When that person chooses to be with someone else, we feel left out.

Often, we are the victim of another's choices or anther's actions or perhaps a mishap that we are powerless to control. When that person does not give us the attention we need, we allow loneliness to claim our attitude and feelings. Loneliness, however, does not depend on a situation in our lives. Loneliness depends on a situation *in our hearts*. Regardless of the circumstance in our lives, we do not have to allow loneliness to control our thoughts. Choosing is a conscious effort. We choose to get out of the house, socialize, meet people and thereby fill that lonely spot in our hearts. If we don't make choices to interact with others, depression could settle in. Depression has a way of making us immobile. We can understand what is right to do, but doing it takes immense effort.

You are filled with this sense of loneliness when your Father God walks up and invites you to another Dance. It is the worst of all possible times. You had much rather just go someplace and cry. What could He possibly say to help you this time? What could He do that would help this intense loneliness?

He begins. "I have a story to tell you. Would you sit by me on this bench while we talk? I think you will know the main character."

You agree, and he begins talking about an ancient story from the Bible. He takes you back, once again, to Hosea.

"Israel had not behaved. They were rebellious and stubborn. They no longer acknowledged Me and all that I had done for them. I withdrew myself from them and sent them into the wilderness. I sent them away from my provisions. I sent them to the desert.

"They thought I was sending them there for punishment, and they were partly right. I had another plan. I actually lured them into the desert so that I could talk to them, love them, restore them, and give them back all that they had lost.

"There is a particular valley called the Valley of Achor. (A-kor) It means the Valley of Trouble. I wanted to lure them to the Valley of Trouble for a specific reason. I wanted to lure them there not to hurt them but to *love them into knowing Me*. I wanted to make their Valley of Trouble a Door of Hope."(Hosea 2:14-15)

You question. "Why would you take them to the desert, to a place of Trouble, and then give them hope there? Why didn't you just give them hope and skip the desert part?

"Oh, but then they would not have wanted my love. They would have had what they wanted and would not have needed Me. No, I have seen it happen again and again. Mankind will not listen to me until they are in the valley. So, I lured them to the valley."

"You actually lured them? How?"

"I made sure they got there. I had to overwhelm Israel's will in order to get it back. I had to take them to a place where they were completely dependent on me. Just like with you, I had to take away so I could give back."

"Like me? You have something to do with my loneliness?"

"I have, in a way the human mind cannot comprehend, brought you to your loneliness for My purposes and reasons. I know if you end up in the desert, I can get your attention. Otherwise you, like all humans, will be too prone to forget I even exist."

"I don't understand why you would lure me to the valley. I'm not a bad person. I try to do the right things. I don't intentionally hurt people. Why me?"

"I see rivers in you that are stagnant, colorful flowers in you that are being choked out by weeds. I see sunshine in you that weeps behind an ominous dark cloud. I see a frightened woman who is missing the Dance of Life because she is afraid to step out and take the first step. I know the potential in you. Glorious possibilities are inside of you. You don't even know what they are. I want to bring all of that out. I want to water your flowers, pluck out the weeds, and clean out your polluted rivers. I don't want you to walk through life with a limp. I want you to walk with joy, move with purpose, face your obstacles with courage and find a life with me that you never even knew existed."

"But, Father," you argue. "It seems like such an awkward twist. If you want me to have all of those things, why don't you just make it happen? Just do it. Why put me in the desert? I can find all of those things away from the desert."

"That is the mistake many of my children make. That's why they are so busy filling their days with those things they *think* will help them. They begin their days with anxiety, maybe taking a pill or two to help them get to work. They move through their days with rat-raced speed, filling the hours in order to avoid the loneliness within, then falling into their beds at night, perhaps with another pill, to escape the loneliness of the night hours. I have better plans for them, if they will only listen."

You think about what He has said. The bench seems to glue you to its embrace and even your wiggling doesn't help. Should you take your Father's hand for this dance?

"Well," He answers. "Why not? You are already in the desert. Why not find out exactly what I am talking about while you are here?"

You decide to take that first step.

"Wonderful," He smiles. "The first step is the hardest. The rest won't be quite as difficult."

A heavenly band begins to play the soft music of a symphony. Beautiful tones blend together as you move onto the Dance Floor. You never thought you would need the Desert Dance. You always thought that kind of dance was for someone else. Here you are in your own desert, desperately needing encouragement. Desperately needing love.

"Your hands are shaking," your Father says. "Are you nervous with Me?"

"Not with You, Father. I'm nervous because I don't know the outcome of my desert. If You brought me here, you have a reason. I'm afraid I won't learn what my reason is, and You'll have to bring me here again. I don't like it here. I don't want to be here this time, and I never want to be here again. After I go through this dance one time, will that be enough? Will that be enough for the rest of my life?"

He smiles, concern and compassion moving all over His face. "Now, my child," your Father lovingly responds, "if I told you the future, your name would be Eve. She wanted to know everything too. She wanted to be as powerful as I am. That was the beginning of her downfall. Because of her desire to be like me, she experienced tremendous suffering. Some things are meant for only Me to know. It is better that way. Can you trust me?"

He continued. "Loneliness, suffering and pain are the tools used to convert the dry dusty dirt roads of your life into the paved highways of growth and wisdom. Dirt roads are harder to walk, more difficult to drive on, and leave dust on your feet or vehicle. Once you get past a dirt road and onto the pavement, the driving goes smoother, there are fewer bumps, and you arrive at your destination a little sooner. I use the paving of a life to smooth away the rocks, pebbles, and stones of your dirt path. I walk beside you during the transition. I watch with loving eyes. I cry when the paving process becomes too difficult. I rescue you before the sun soaks into your pavement with too much heat. The process is not easy. Once you're there, you gaze back at your Paved Road and smile. You feel complete and happy. Life begins."

You pout. "I'm fine with being a dirt road."

"Oh, but I'm *not* fine with that. Why should I let you stay that way when I know what is needed to bring you true happiness? You were made to be a princess route; not a horse and buggy path. I made you. I know what potential is inside of you. Only I know what is needed to change you."

Your hand relaxes, but only a little. The thoughts are scary. Is your Father saying that this intense pain, this loneliness, this desert time could possibly be repeated again? You take a deep breath and sigh.

The Dance Floor of Life is large and overwhelming. Just thinking of the length of this dance wearies you. You haven't the energy to move much.

It's too long. Overpowering. Intimidating. You are sure life will completely pass you by while you stay in the Desert Dance.

"How long will this dance take, Father?"

"That depends," He answers.

"On what? On whether or not my circumstances change?"

"No."

"Well, then, on whether or not a friend comes into my life and offers help?"

"No."

"Well, maybe it depends on you? You decide how long it will take me?"

"No."

You are exasperated. "What, then?"

"It depends on the Desert Dance. It depends on where the Dance takes you."

"Where it takes me? What do you mean?"

"Just rest in my embrace and move with my music. You'll see."

It seems you dance for hours, but you cannot relax. This dance drains your energy. Your feet become weary, and you find it difficult to even move your feet to the next step. Your arms feel heavy, and your back begins to hurt. You are so tired. You see a large sign on the wall: "The Work of the Desert." You understand. This dance is not a dance of ease.

You see another door. The sign over it reads, "Manna Multiplied."

You have to ask. "Manna Multiplied? What is that?"

"Why don't we move through that door and find out," your Father suggests.

As soon as you go through the door, the sky fills with white snow. "Snow?" you ask.

"Why snow? It's not even cold? Wait. It isn't snow."

"No, it's manna," Your Father answers. "Taste and eat. It will satisfy your soul and give you necessary fuel to keep going."

You gather a handful. Sweet, honey wafers melt in your mouth, and you feel nourishment moving throughout your body. Energy returns. You feel strong again.

"I always supply manna in the desert," your Father says. "Always."

You continue the dance, but you are wondering. What does He mean when He says that the end of this Dance depends on where the Dance takes you? Instead of worrying about it, you close your eyes and decide to allow the movement of His Dance to flow inside of you.

You see another door. Over it is written "The Door of Hope." You remember your Father talking about that when you sat together on the bench. You glance up at His face. Does He see it, too? Will He guide you to this Door? You are ready for it. Your feet are tired once more, and your energy has left. You are ready for some Hope.

As quickly as you think it, you are there. As He takes you through this door, a comfortable feeling envelops you as a bright light shines before you. With every step, the light continues, and you move as if you have on new shoes. You don't understand it, but you feel it. New life begins to surge into your veins, and you are renewed. Without knowing how, Hope moves into your heart, then to your mind and then to your will. You decide you will gather hope to your heart just as you gathered the manna.

Your Father looks down at you. "You are learning the lesson of the desert, my daughter. You are gleaning from the Work of the Desert. Your Valley of Trouble has become a Door of Hope. You are different. Look down at your feet."

You look, and the shoes you had on are gone. Instead, you have new shoes. "What is this all about, Father?"

"These are called the shoes that carry you from where you have been to where you are going. They only come off if you decide to take them off. Otherwise, they will remain. They only come to those who grow through the Desert Dance, those who move through the Dance, receive the manna to keep going, and then walk through the Door of Hope. You have done this, my daughter."

As quickly as He says it, He is gone. You stand alone, engulfed in blazing light, new shoes on your feet and new energy in your soul. You hear a voice. "Continue the dance."

"Alone? All by myself?"

"Yes. You can do it. You are no longer in the Desert Dance. You have moved through the Door of Hope. Dance. Keep dancing. Hope will dance with you."

You feel a bit foolish, but since no one is there to watch, you begin to slowly sway to the music. You move lightly but resolutely. Each step is easier than the one before. Hope changes you. You are looking away from the Desert as you move all around the dance floor, twisting, smiling, and even laughing. Is this the same person? You aren't lonely anymore. You aren't lonely because you are finding meaning for your life, even if no one else is around to share it. No one else *is* around; yet, you are not alone.

In a way that only God can do, He leaves so you can move inside of your new Hope, yet He stays so that He is still close by. You feel Him. As surely as you felt Him when you danced, you feel Him now. He becomes your Hope. He becomes your Joy. He becomes everything you need to make it through loneliness when it comes to rest at your door again. Now you know the secret. You know what to do.

You know because you've lived it. You are no longer afraid of what will happen if loneliness comes again. If called to the desert again, you can make it. You know you can. You are called Princess. You are called His daughter. You are called a paved road. You are called brave and strong and capable.

The dance goes on. Forever. The Door of Hope moves all over the Dance Floor of your Life. Where you go, it goes. You just have to notice it. Manna continues to come. You just have to taste it. Life has purpose again.

The strangest thing happens. You begin thanking your Father for the Desert Dance. Without it, you would never have tasted manna. Without it, you would never have found your Door of Hope.

You hear a voice behind you. "Was it worth it? Was it worth loneliness to find new life?"

You don't hesitate. Instead you bow and gratefully answer. "Yes. It is worth whatever I have to go through in order to find new life with you. It is worth the loneliness in order to discover the sweetness of your desert food. It is worth the pain to know the peace. Thank you Father. Thank you for the Desert Dance."

To My Reader: None of us will escape the desert. There will be those times when we feel intense loneliness and grief, and our lives seem to be engulfed with pain. Without this experience, you will never find the Door of Hope. Are you in a desert now? Hold your Father's hand through the Desert Dance. He has a whole house full of Hope Doors. He has one just for you.

Prayer: Dear Father, you are my Hope. On days when I don't realize that, remind me. Take me through that door, even when I don't understand why I'm there in the first place. Teach me to trust you even when I question. Thank you for loving me enough to dance with me in my trouble, to hold me in my loneliness, to never leave me in my pain. You are the God of all hope, all comfort and of all my desert days. AMEN.

Chapter Eighteen

Dance of Holiness
(It Can Happen For You)

Your day has just begun when you hear the beautiful sounds of a full orchestra. Each note comes as if it has been magically drawn from instruments that know innately what to play. Marvelous, vibrant music fills your head. The blend is one you have never heard before. Something about this music makes you know you cannot stay seated. As rich tones fill the room, you instinctively know that you must stand. Just as you cannot sit still when you hear songs about your native land, neither can you sit still now. You rise. You close your eyes, and suddenly your hands lift into the air.

You are alone, yet surrounded by majesty. How can you explain this to others? You cannot. The glory of the moment saturates your soul, and you close your eyes in wonder. Your Father God has been loving you into knowing Him in so many delightfully wonderful ways. He has showered you with the blessings of kingdom living as He poured His love into you. What is today's message? What are these wonderful, majestic orchestra sounds all about?

Sinking deep within your spirit are these words, "Be holy because I am holy." (Leviticus 11:44) For a moment, you falter, bringing your arms back to your side and opening your eyes wide. Holy? Of course, you realize *God* is holy, but what is this you are hearing? *You* are to be holy, too? How? How can humanity and holiness reside in the same person? Can that happen?

A soft voice whispers in your spirit. "It happened with Jesus."

"Oh sure," you think to yourself. "Of *course,* Jesus. No other being can expect holiness to enter into a mere human's life. That only happened once. Only once in this world did divinity enter humanity. Isn't that right?"

Silence. As you wait for some kind of answer, your Father arrives.

"Oh, Father. I'm so glad you came. I have a question."

"That's why I came. I have an answer."

"I have these thoughts running through me this morning that I am to be holy. I know this idea cannot be from you. Only you are holy, right? Only Jesus and you?"

"Not exactly. Only Jesus and I are *divine*, but *holiness* is available to everyone.

Come. Let me take you once again to life's dance and teach you about the Dance of Holiness."

No, thank you. Your Father is asking the impossible, so you decline the offer. You'd better stay away from this dance. No sense in even trying. You already know you will fail before you even begin.

Once more, the compelling presence of the Dance Teacher overcomes your defenses. Slowly, you walk to the floor.

The same melodious sounds bounce into your heart, like an echo that will never end. As you are thinking of all of the reasons you cannot do this dance, the music overpowers your thoughts. It is simply beautiful. You begin to get caught up in what appears to be a never-ending, magical moment. Thoughts of making a mistake begin to move out of your head. All you can hear, all you can think about, is the music of this dance. Your heavenly Father holds you closely. Then, a strange thing happens.

You blend into Him in such a way that you cannot tell where you end and He begins. With your intellect, you know two of you are dancing, but within your spirit, you feel a strange, yet intriguing and comforting oneness with your Father. How can this be? Two of you are dancing, yet only one. His soothing voice comes from Him, and yet it is within you.

"All I have is yours. And all you have is mine." (John 17:10)

"I remember reading these words. They are from Jesus," I respond. "They are from Jesus to God. They don't apply to *me*, do they?"

"All I have is yours. And all you have is mine."

"I don't understand. How can a conversation between you and your Son ever be applied to me?"

The answer stirs within you as you continue to blend as one. "If my character and presence truly live within you, then you will reflect Me. If my holiness dwells within your spirit, then you will reflect Me. A life lived in holiness is a life set apart for my purposes. This can only happen when you desire to leave all else and come to My Dance of Holiness."

You don't say a word because you know if you do, it will come out wrong. Your thoughts, however, are centered on what you do each day and how that can possibly be called holy. Life happens fast. You have many responsibilities, and you don't want to miss anything going on in your home, your job, or your community. Being holy sounds like anything but fun. You still have a lot of joy for life inside of you. You're not ready to pull away into a monastic style of living!

"I'm not calling you to a monastery."

You are nervous. You completely forgot that your Father knows everything you are thinking, so you try to back up.

"Well, it's not that. It's just that I don't feel I can make it on this particular dance. I'll do some of the others. I want to, in fact. This one seems to call for me to have to be perfect, and I just can't go there. Holiness and perfection are the same, right?"

"We'll talk about perfection a little later. Holiness is being set apart. For now, I want you to realize that when I called you as My own, on to My Dance Floor of Life, I called you to be set apart. That means, if you are serious about your walk with Me, you will indeed want to live a life steeped in piety."

"Wait a minute, now. I don't want *anything* to do with being pious. That sounds like someone who sticks her nose in the air and walks around with a "better than you" attitude."

"Piety simply means that you are set apart for devotion to Me. You have a zeal for Me, a hunger for Me. This hunger ends in holiness. You pull apart from those things that have pulled you down into the world, and as you pull closer and closer to me, you are pulled up away from those cares that have held you captive. Piety is a conscious choice to live for me. Piety and Holiness walk hand in hand. I desire for you to live a life of Piety."

The music slows down, and you continue to feel that same Oneness with your heavenly Father. You dance slowly and methodically, each step reminding you of its clear call. The music is invigorating and also challenging. You know that you can never dance this dance alone. You need help. The call to a life of piety is a call to separate yourself from certain people and some habits that you have held dear. To give them up will be difficult. You're not too sure you want to continue this dance.

"I know," your Father lovingly says as He continues moving you to the rhythm of the music. "I know exactly what you are feeling. Can you trust me that this dance will be the dance that can change your life? This dance will move you from being a Christian of slight commitment to a Christian of deeper commitment. More is waiting for you, my beloved. You have only tasted a small portion of what I have in store for you. It's like you have tasted the milk, but I want to turn the milk into the tastiest ice cream you've ever had, with rich whipped cream on top. I want to give you the best. I can do that if you will decide to draw away from this world and live a life of holiness with me. I have set you apart for sacred use. Come, feel the dance with me. Allow yourself to flow into my holiness."

Something about this offer is appealing and yet frightening. You're not ready for all your fun to be taken away. You're not ready for this kind of deep commitment.

Your Father interrupts your thoughts, "It is impossible to be neutral."

You become defensive. "I'm not neutral," you insist. "I have given my heart to you. I've been baptized. I go to church. I certainly belong more to you than to the world. I think I'm okay. I really do. I think I'm just fine."

"Then why are you on the dance floor with me? Why are you staying for the Dance of Holiness?"

You don't have an answer. The strength of your Father's grip on you as you dance together brings you such peace. If holiness spawns peace in your life, then maybe it's not such a bad idea after all. It sounds impossible, yet the music has a fascinating rhythm of pure love. You can't leave the dance floor even if you want to. You are captivated by this dance.

His radiant, deep, yet soft and mellow voice continues. "The distinctive mark of my people is not wealth, prosperity, or prestige. It is holiness. Holiness comes as my children sincerely desire to obey Me and become devoted to Me."

"I don't know how to get there. What do I have to do? It sounds so hard."

"In my Book, I wrote through the author of Hebrews these words, 'But when this priest (My Son, Jesus) had offered for all time one sacrifice for sins, (His death on the cross) He sat down at the right hand of God (Me). Since that time, He waits for His enemies to be made his footstool, because by one sacrifice He has made perfect forever those who are being made holy.' (Hebrews 10:12-14)

"You asked me earlier about perfection. I see you as perfect, though you still have the propensity to sin. Because of what My Son did on the cross, through His blood, I see *you* as perfect. Perfect means that when I look at you, I see you as perfectly fitted to do My will. You have everything you need, because you have My Son's sacrifice. You will still make mistakes until that final day when I call you Home with me forever. With My Son's power living in you, you are perfectly able to do all that I need you to do in order for My Kingdom to come. When you accept My Son, from that minute on, I see you as perfectly fit to serve Me.

"Holiness is progressive. In your walk with me, you are being progressively set apart for My special use. My people should not be surprised that holiness is a process. All of my children still need to grow in some area of their lives. Holiness is a daily decision that claims a continual growth in My Ways, My Life,

My Habits, My Temperament, My Disposition, My Outlook, My Faith."

You think carefully before you ask this next question. "You mean I can dance the Dance of Holiness and yet not actually be completely holy?"

"That's the *only* way to dance this dance, my daughter. I'm not finished with you yet. Coming to the Dance of Holiness brings you closer and closer each day into Me."

You feel lighter. Relieved. Thankful.

"Whew. I thought I had to get there first before I could even begin to come to this Dance."

Your Father smiles at you. "Don't you think I know human nature? I made you. I know you live in a very real world with very real pulls on your spiritual life."

"Then tell me how? How do I even begin to 'get there?'"

"Look to My Word. Apply Scripture to all areas of your life. Accept the discipline and guidance My Son provides. Give total control over to Him."

"What you just said made me think you know I can't do this 'total control' thing."

"Oh, you can. Yes, indeed you can. If you'll stay in the Dance of Holiness, you will be able to draw from My Strength when you feel yourself slipping away. It's not a question of whether or not you will slip. You will. It's a question of whether or not you believe my Dance, will stay with Me, and will let me help you when you do."

You are beginning to understand. You look at your feet and realize you still cannot remember where

His feet stop and yours begin. This dance completely sweeps you into Him. The experience is incredibly uplifting, and you are beginning to see the pull of this dance as something you want. Once you work through the fact that you will always live in a human nature and will therefore always be human, you can better accept the call of holiness. You see holiness now as a daily call to be set apart, to make a decision to be devoted to your Father for His special use, and to also consciously decide to be set apart from sin and its influence.

"You seem to want holiness now, but I want to make sure you understand something. You cannot become holy on your own. You don't get there through human effort, struggle or determination. You'll have my Spirit to always help you. He is available always.

"Ah, my daughter. This is what I've been waiting for."

"This? This what?"

"I feel your muscles relaxing and your tense body giving over to My guidance. This, my child, is holiness."

Something inside of you softens. You do feel relaxed. Your defenses have been depleted and your guard is down.

"I think I want this, Father. I think I really, really want this."

"I knew that all along."

"You did? How?"

"Because you are mine. I formed you. I made you. I called you to be set aside for My purposes. I placed this desire within you while you were still in the womb. I knew that one day you would understand."

"Thank you, Father. Keep me where you want me. Hold me tight. I want to be holy as you are holy. I understand it all now."

The dance continues. You are not ready to stop. He reminds you that you never have to, so you stay. Everything else is momentarily forgotten. This is where true Life can be found. In the arms of your Father, everything makes sense.

To My Reader: Holiness doesn't make you better, kinder, happier or even easier to get along with. Holiness does one thing. Holiness sets you apart for service. That's it. In the process, you might become better, kinder and happier, but those attributes are not the goal of holiness. The goal is that you get to *know Him*. The emphasis is on *Him*, not you. May your search for holiness lead you to the end of *yourself* and the beginning of *Himself* in yourself. That's the goal.

Prayer: Kind Father, make me holy as you are holy. Set me apart for your purposes. Use me for your glory. Hold me away from my own needs and point to the need I have for you. Only you. In your Son's Name, Amen.

Chapter Nineteen

A Gentleman's Dance

An understanding of the Holy Spirit is still a far-away concept. Vague. Out of reach. Beyond your comprehension. What exactly is the Holy Spirit?

As you settle into a morning of drinking coffee and relaxing in your favorite chair, you open your Bible and move to the pages that talk about the Spirit of God. As soon as you begin, He appears. Your Father moves to your side, and you know from past dances, that your comprehension will now take on new meaning, without the limitations that stifle your human understanding. Instead, He will give you heavenly understanding. You are ready. Someone has told you that the Spirit is the power you need in your life. You want to know more.

"And that's a very good place to begin," your Father says. "Wanting to know more. You are in a place of hunger. That's the only place to start. Let me introduce you to the third part of my Trinity."

You listen as He explains the Holy Spirit as being the part of God that moves freely and uninhibited into the lives of believers. Because He is Spirit, He can do that. Jesus, as God inhabited in one human body, was not able to crawl inside all other human bodies. That was impossible. He was unable to physically get inside of them and thereby bring His Life to them, but the Holy Spirit can. He is Spirit. He waits for His chance to serve, His chance to move among humans, entering us and teaching us about the nature and heart of God, as seen through Jesus the Christ, our Messiah.

In the Old Covenant, God sent the Holy Spirit at specific times. He came, rested upon someone, anointed him or her in a particular way, and then left. He had not yet been assigned the privilege of dwelling in all believers.

Jesus told His followers to wait for power before they attempted to tell others about Him. After Jesus' resurrection, that is exactly what they did. A group of believers were crowded into one room, waiting for further instructions from the risen Christ. Jesus knew that the Gospel story would fall on deaf ears unless the ones telling the story were empowered. He planned to send His Spirit, the third part of the Trinity, to accomplish this purpose.

As they waited, something magnificent happened. In a supernatural occurrence that cannot be understood with human minds, the Holy Spirit descended upon those gathered and appeared as wind, fire and power. (Acts 2) As if they were drunk, they staggered down the stairs and into the streets, telling those who had gathered from many countries about God and His great plans. Crowds had come to Jerusalem for the annual Feast of Pentecost, for the purpose of praising God for the harvest. They listened because those empowered were talking in a language they could understand, and another harvest began to grow. The harvest of the first church! The Holy Spirit supernaturally enabled each person to speak in the native language of those gathered in Jerusalem that day. Because they heard the message of God in *their* language by people who didn't even speak their language, they too were filled with joy and went back to their homes with an exciting, miraculous story to tell. *Jesus is alive. He has risen. He has given us an assignment.* They were to welcome His Spirit into their spirits, giving the Holy Spirit freedom to teach them about Jesus so that they could teach the rest of the world. Jesus knew that mere humans could not accomplish this task without His Spirit. He came to them as their Helper, their Comforter and their Encourager, just to name a few.

On that day, the Holy Spirit breathed spiritual fire on those first followers and enabled them to preach a bold message of salvation. From then on, they were so sure of His resurrection, so sure of Him, that they began to take little thought of their own needs in submission to the needs of a sin-sick world. They preached with fervor. They baptized new converts. They placed their hands on the sick and brought divine healing. They learned to get along in a community of folks with different personalities, with some they might not have even liked. They didn't always agree on theory or method, but they did agree on purpose, zeal and passion. Their spirits were set afire. They wanted to win the world for Christ. Because of their excitement, accompanied by joy, they were able to begin the church Christ came to establish.

Those first disciples learned that the Holy Spirit could be in many places at one time. He is not confined by space or time. He chooses to come into a life and bring the power of the living God. He is, after all, God's power moving into believers everywhere. His purpose is to bring *new life* as He explodes *His Life* over this earth.

Those who walk through roads of pain and end up in the Valley of Trouble, forced flat down on their backs, are finally able to look up and see the Spirit's desire to help. Those who have danced life's dance alone, forcing their views, pushing for their rights, stepping on others to get ahead but getting nowhere, are those who might finally recognize their senseless endeavors and see their need for the companionship of the Holy Spirit. Complacent minds and hearts of apathy will never know His help. Strength comes as we move past self-sufficiency into recognition of our need for more than we presently have.

The Holy Spirit will never force entrance into our lives. He is a Gentleman who awaits your invitation. If you are a believer and have invited Christ into your life, then the Holy Spirit has already entered you. If the God-Trio has been invited inside and you have welcomed Him to live in you, then you already have the Trio in you. You have God the Father, God the Son, and God the Holy Spirit. You have God as ruler, Creator and Judge. You have the Son as risen Savior and Redeemer. You have the Holy Spirit. However, the Spirit's gentlemanly Nature prevents His entrance of *full control* by any other way except by invitation. He is there, in you, yet waiting for you to let Him expand into all of your life. He sits in your heart with your Savior, making sure you are indeed assured of your place in eternity. That is settled when you invite Christ in and recognize His rightful place in your life. All the while the Holy Spirit is sitting on a button called "Go," the button you will push when you tell Him to stop sitting in the background and come to the forefront of your life. The *Go Button* can only be pushed by you. He is that Gentleman who will wait until you tell him you are ready. Sometimes He moves to the edge of that button, so eager for you to let Him move into your whole life. Sometimes He sees you as "almost ready for Go;" yet, your will remains in control. He knows you don't understand the full implication of giving up so that He can take over. You are scared. You fear you will lose all your ability to control your own thought patterns, your decisions. You forget, however, that you are dealing with a Gentleman. He never forces. He only takes control of what you tell Him He can control. Once you realize that, you will want His power operating in you.

Why do you need the Holy Spirit? Because your prayer life will take on wings of flight and move with speed to the heavenlies. Guidance will come.

Peace will accompany the guidance. Your heart's desires will combine with His heart's desires, and you will see mountains beginning to move. Scripture you thought was dull will now become meaningful to you. In other words, you will walk daily with the Comforter, this Helper and Guide who wants to move with you into all areas of your life. Can you stifle Him or quench Him once He has begun? Yes, you can. He remains a Gentleman until you move from this life to the next, but once you know Him and the power of His glory, you will never want to diminish His power. You will guard this priceless commodity with everything in you. You will ask for His help in fighting off every trick of the devil.

You ask the obvious. "How do I give the Holy Spirit freedom in my life? How do I welcome this Gentleman?"

"You have only to ask. You ask for Him to fill you and flow out of you in new ways. You tell Him you are moving *self over* so that He can *move all over*. You invite Him to be not just the Savior of your life but also the Lord of your life. You welcome His companionship and gratefully look forward to the journey of knowing Him better.

"The Gentleman comes to you as a soft reminder daily of the life He has for you. He respects you enough not to barge in. He hopes you respect Him enough to let Him enter in His own gentle way. He longs for you to trust Him enough to surrender complete control of your life to Him."

You sit there, taking all of this in, excited about the possibilities of a daily walk with this Gentleman.

Your Father God says something to you now that you had never thought of.

"You do realize, don't you my child, that what you and I are doing is what the world calls prayer? Prayer is simply engaging in conversation with me. Both of us get to talk. It's been my turn. Now it is yours."

Prayer? This has been prayer? You realize you've never known prayer like this. You have always done all of the talking. You didn't know God wanted a chance. So you begin.

"Father, this is what I have needed for so long and did not know it."

He answers, "Yes. Many of My children sit in church every Sunday, not understanding this. They have never heard about the Gentleman. They feel, because they have accepted my Son, they have all they need. No one has explained to them that there is more that will lead to an abundant and full life."

You wonder. Now that you know, how can you be satisfied with anything less?

Is this what is meant by *loving me into knowing you?* It is God's love that brings me to His side? Is it God's love that holds me there?

"That's right. I don't operate in any other way. My plan all along is to love you so much that you will want to know Me and will want to love Me back. All of your life, I am busy with My love-plan for each of my children. The enemy constantly gets in the way. He discourages and destroys. He wounds and kills. He wants to make My greatest creation, mankind, think they must bow down to him and that they have no other choice. He is sneaky, conniving and highly convincing. Every day, as he throws his hard balls at my children, I'm catching them as quickly as I can, trying to keep my children out of danger. He will never win, but he makes many think that he will. Some get discouraged and sometimes give up on life. I have a love-plan for them, but they only see the darkness of Satan's defeat."

You like what you hear. A new trickle of excitement begins to form inside. Life with the Holy Spirit sounds convincing, intriguing, and desirable. "How do I get there? What do I have to do?"

"You simply need to want the Gentleman to dance with you more than you want to dance alone. You want to desire the Holy Spirit enough to ask Him to claim your life in a full and rich way. You submit your desires to His. He is such a Gentleman that He never emphasizes Himself. He always reminds you of what Jesus has done for you. *The Holy Spirit alone does in us what Jesus did for us*." (Oswald Chambers, *Biblical Ethics*, Christian Literature Crusade, 1947, p. 99)

You place your hand in His and stand to begin A Gentleman's Dance. Maybe you have not known too many gentlemen in your life, but now you want to know this One. You wonder how it will feel to be around a Gentleman who knows how to treat a lady. Everything about this feels right. As you and your Father God walk to the Dance Floor of Life you are suddenly aware that you cannot see Him any more. He has become the third part of the God-Head. He is Spirit. You don't see Him, but you know He is there, guiding your steps, gently moving you to the right or left as you swirl all around the floor. To others, you appear to be dancing alone.

"Holy Spirit, I want this Dance with You. I want to know that as I move through life, You will move with me. I want the power to live inside of this world with a victory that can only come as You take over in my life."

You relax, feeling the strength of the Spirit's hand as you continue the Dance. You feel joy and peace in a way that has eluded you before. You never want to leave this Dance. The good news is that you do not have to leave. You get to stay. You simply move the Dance Floor into your home, your work, and your yard. The Dance goes with you as you get dressed in the morning, as you eat your meals, as you drive your car and as you interact with others. True to His nature, the Gentleman stays. He will always be with you. What immeasurable joy is yours when you give Him free movement into every part of your life. Your Christian walk, from this time forward, does not have to be controlled by your own efforts or by a "have to do this" attitude. Instead, you will want to live as completely with Him as you can. You will hunger to read the Bible. You will desire to be a part of a community of worship. You will want to forgive others and live in humility. You will want to hand Him your hand as you get out of your bed each morning and hold that same hand as you move throughout your day. The good news is He stays. The Gentleman stays.

Even though you are a lady walking with a Gentleman, it's quite all right if you shout an exuberant *Hallelujah!*

To My Reader: Are you looking for a Gentleman to stand by your side as you move throughout the struggles of your life? The Holy Spirit wants to be that Gentleman. He will gently love you through all that you face. Once you really meet Him, you will never want to let go of His hand. He will be the One who moves you into a deeper walk with your Savior and who reminds you of how much your Father God loves you. If you need a prayer to help you invite Him to be your constant Companion, I would like to offer one.

Prayer: Holy Spirit, I invite you to come into your fullness in my life. I invite you to be a part of everything I do. I ask you to come into the struggling parts of my day in such a way that I actually hear you talking to me, guiding me, giving me advice. I love that you love me enough to want to dance this dance with me. The lady I am responds to the Gentleman you are. Come, Holy Spirit. I need you. Amen.

Chapter Twenty

Dance of Trust

A friend taught me a prayer that I love and have passed on to others. "Lord, open doors no man can shut, and close doors no man can open." It takes a total trust in God to pray a prayer like that. It simply means, "I trust you, God. You are in charge of this situation. I know what I want, but I'm asking that you close that door if it is wrong. Slam it so tight that no man can open it, but if this situation is right for me, (or my loved one) then please open it so wide that no human hand can close it."

I have prayed for certain situations that fit this category. But, for the life of me, I cannot understand why God won't just crack the door and allow my prayer request to be granted. The request seems okay to me. It sounds right. Feels right. Yet, the door of that request seems sealed shut with concrete, with an electric wire that shocks me if I try to turn the knob. Above that door, a "Do Not Enter" sign blinks on and off, and a siren goes off if I try to gently push on the door. Everything about that door is barricaded to me. It will not budge. The door simply will not open. He has definitely closed this door, and no man can open it.

What I *should do* when the door won't budge is fall on my face and yell **Thank you** as loudly as I can. God is protecting me from something! He has reasons to close that particular door. He has something better in mind. In my shortsighted vision, I simply cannot see what He sees. Isaiah 55:8 says, "My thoughts are not your thoughts, nor are my ways your ways."

Again and again, God tries to let us know that we cannot fit Him into our mold. We cannot make His plans conform to our plans. We cannot decide what we want to happen and then stamp "God's will" on it. He doesn't work that way. He reserves the right to withhold answers to certain prayer requests. The hard cold reality of this is that God does not owe us an explanation. If He thinks it's best to shut the door, He will shut it. If He thinks it's best to open it, He will fling it wide open! He doesn't need our permission to do either.

The Dance of Trust is a difficult dance. It requires giving up something you want. You give up your right to make all the decisions and hold on to God's right to do what He knows is best. When I go on the dance floor with my Heavenly Father for the Dance of Trust, I go with a struggle. I dig my feet into the dance floor and try with all of my might to pull away. I want to be in control of the answer to my request. I don't want to let it go. Trusting is hard work! To put my dreams, wishes and desires totally into the arms of God is not something I can easily do. I know with my mind that God knows best. I even say it with my lips to others. Actually *doing it* is something else! Why? Because I know that His answer might not be what I want to hear, and in my self-determined nature that I inherited from Eve (see, she always comes up!) I feel I really know best how to handle my own life.

When I was a girl, my earthly father taught me how to ride a bicycle. Even now, I remember him running along the side of my bike, encouraging me, telling me I could do it. I fell a lot, and he helped me get back up. I scraped my knees, and he washed them off. Somehow, with his encouragement, I finally began to trust the process of allowing the pedals to hold me securely on the bike. I remember my handle-bars wiggling so much that I thought I would never get my bike moving in a straight line. Over and over I tried. Over and over, my father stayed by my side, running with me.

I not only had to trust the pedals and my ability to steer correctly, but I had to trust my father. I had to trust that he really thought I could do this. I had to trust that what he said would eventually happen.

"You can do this, Baby Jo! Keep trying. You're getting it. Don't give up!"

It would have been easier at times for me to just forget the whole thing and walk everywhere! I guess you could say I abandoned my will and gave it over to my father. I believed in him. He believed in me. He said I could do this. His trust in me eventually made me trust myself enough to finally take off in faith and begin my childhood enjoyment of riding bicycles.

When I am praying about something that I want to happen, and it doesn't happen, sometime it would be easier for me to just forget about that prayer concern and give up. That's not what God wants. What He wants is my trust. He runs along beside me saying, "You can do this. Keep trying. You're getting it. Don't give up."

Eventually, I have to abandon my will to God's will. He believes I can. He trusts me to take off on a new road of faith, one that is unsure to my way of thinking, but very sure to Him. My handlebars are shaking, but He knows what is going to happen if I abandon my will to His. He has my best interest in mind. I don't understand. I may never understand. He has never told me that understanding is something I will have.

Look at Job in the Bible. He lost everything and naturally questioned all that happened to him. God never gave him a reason. Instead, He reminded Job of who He was. Through the realization that God was sovereign and Job wasn't, Job finally accepted that he would never get understanding, but he did need to get trust.

Proverbs 3:5-6 says, "Trust in the Lord with all your heart and lean not on your own understanding; in all your ways acknowledge Him and He will direct your path."

This verse doesn't say, "Trust in the Lord when you feel like it." It doesn't say, "Trust in the Lord if you have nothing better planned." It says, "Trust Him." I am not to lean on my own understanding because I will lose my balance doing that. I will fall down. I can only lean so far into my own abilities, but nothing secure is there to hold on to. I don't have the answers. I never will. Some circumstances are so broad and so deep that if I lean on my own understanding, I will end up discouraged and disappointed.

I don't lean on my own understanding when I turn on my computer. If I had to lean on my understanding before I touched the "on" button, I would never use the computer. I don't understand how a computer works. The mystery of how it works does not, however, keep me from using it. I count on daily e-mails of communication. I use my computer for all my writing purposes. I would limit myself tremendously if I had to understand the computer before I turned it on. I trust the computer to blink my blank screen into life every morning. I trust it to find information for me and to relay messages from me. I don't even think about understanding how a computer works. I just abandon myself to its magnificent ability to connect with resources I would never find on my own.

I have more difficulty abandoning myself and my situations to God. Why? Why can't I just abandon myself to His magnificent ability to connect with resources I would never find on my own? He has every resource available. He knows what I need and when I need it. Yet, as I move on the dance floor for the Dance of Trust, I hesitate, trying to find something else to do or somewhere else to go, and thus avoid this dance. It is too hard.

When I think about it, I use trust in unknown circumstances every single day of my life. If I didn't, I would never get out of the bed. I trust my car to take me safely where I need to go. I trust the caution lights to stop traffic so I can move forward. I trust the breakfast food I buy at the drive-through on my way to work. I trust that somebody who loved me yesterday still loves me today. I trust people, places, things, and circumstances of my life. Yet, I have trouble trusting God with my life.

"Father," I say. "I really do want you to close doors that no man can open and open doors that no man can close. It's just so hard to let go of some situations and turn them over to you. I need your help."

Oswald Chambers says, "God is never in a panic, nothing can be done that He is not absolute Master of and no one in earth or heaven can shut a door He has opened, nor open a door He has shut. God alters the inevitable when we get in touch with Him." (Oswald Chambers, *If Thou Will Be Perfect* Christian Literature Crusade, Fort Washington, Pennsylvania, 1941)

I am learning that this Dance of Trust is ongoing. I think I have mastered it. Then another prayer need comes before me, and I have to learn it all over again, especially with prayer needs of my family. I have to believe in the Dance even when I don't want to. I have to know God is working for the good of all concerned even when I don't understand.

A popular saying these days is that "God is good, all the time. And all the time, God is good." I saw that belief demonstrated in my mother. All her life, she showed me that God is good. She moved forward through difficulties with great faith and resolve. I never heard her complain or murmur about anything. My mother was known for a kind, gentle, and non-condemning spirit.

Mama had to take care of my daddy after he was paralyzed from a stroke. He never walked again after that, but worse than the immobility of his body was the immobility of his mind. My daddy's bright mind diminished before Mother's eyes. With his keen business sense, he had always taken care of the details of taxes, rental houses, financial savings, and other financial matters. Now, in her eighties, my mother had to learn. She wanted to ask him for help, but it was useless. Fortunately, my sister inherited my father's ability to work with numbers, so she and her husband assisted Mother with this overwhelming task. Still, Mother did her homework and learned all she needed to keep Daddy's affairs in order.

A stroke leaves a person completely dehuman-ized. He has to give up all privacy and is forced to depend on others. I watched my mother as she patiently and lovingly dealt with Daddy's refusal to eat, his lack of motivation to cooperate with the therapists, and his need for daily caretakers to do for him what he had always done for himself. Mother put aside everything she wanted for eight years in order to serve him unselfishly. The husband he used to be would have bragged on her, encouraged her, and comforted her. The husband he was now could not do any of those things. The husband he had been would not have stopped complimenting her cooking. Now, he rebelled, made a face, and spit out some of her cooking. He seemed unaware of all of her efforts, and completely ungrateful. Of course, he could not help that. The stroke had stolen almost every emotion except his will to be stubborn. She handled even that with great love and patience.

My mother was a devoted Christian. I'm sure she asked God many times to open this door for my daddy. I asked her how she handled all of these changes.

She said, "I take all I can take. Then, I slip into a room by myself, and I cry."

God never opened that door for her. Daddy eventually died of complications from the stroke, but she never once questioned God's plan. She didn't feel she had to know why He closed that door and never healed Daddy.

My mother taught me so many things in my lifetime. One of her greatest teachings came through her silence. She taught me quiet acceptance. She taught me that complaining would accomplish nothing, and that no matter what, God still reigns. She would never have imagined questioning God.

When I finally submit to God's Dance of Trust, I think of my mother. She went to heaven seven years after Daddy, and I wish I could talk to her about how it must have felt to see Daddy whole and happy and in his right mind again. She probably would tell me that God knows the doors He has to close and has His reasons. She would probably tell me that she learned so much during Daddy's years of sickness, and that she has learned even more about God's ways since she now lives in His heaven.

I'm sure my mama would tell me to keep the dance. She would tell me that she understands it all now, and that some day, I will too.

The Dance of Trust holds me tightly. As I face each difficult situation in my life or in the life of someone I love, I know I have to ask that prayer my friend taught me and that my mother illustrated. "Lord, shut doors that no man can open and open doors that no man can shut." I may not understand, but then it wouldn't be called The Dance of Trust.

To My Reader: Trusting God begins with an act of our will. We decide to trust. We understand that situations in our life are far bigger than anything we can handle, so through an act of our will, we turn to Him. Once you have some experience with this, trusting will become easier. Think of it this way. Can you trust the One who died for you? Can you trust Him to work in your behalf on all of your heart's concerns? If you and I cannot trust Him, then we cannot trust anyone. He is the Friend who will never leave you nor forsake you. He will never let you down. Maybe the following prayer will help you get started.

Prayer: Father, the burdens I am carrying are too big for me, yet I don't feel that anyone can handle them besides me. Trusting you to take care of this is very hard. I feel I have to *do* something, *say* something, *repair* something in order to find a suitable solution. But, you are asking me to give this to you and then go on about my daily life, trusting that you can handle it. I'm not too good at this, but I want to try. Please help me. In your Son's Name I pray, Amen.

Epilogue

When I was a freshman in college, a well-meaning preacher placed a loving slap on my back and asked, "BJ, do you love the Lord?" I was speechless. Love the Lord? I found that question to be a strange one. Did He love me? Yes, I was sure of it. But, did I love Him? I had never thought about it. His question actually intimidated me and made me very uncomfortable. My heavenly Father was standing by me that day, recognizing my limitations and joyfully thinking of the day I would strengthen the covenant I had with Him, a covenant that would claim intimacy as its banner. Intimacy would eventually bring knowing Him to the surface. Later in my life, loving God would become as natural to me as breathing. I just had to cross over some rocky paths to get there.

I am sure that many of you reading this book will find, even after you've read the last chapter, that intimacy with God still seems like a vague concept. I hope you will give the thoughts in this book time to digest and time to move all through your spirit. If you will make an attempt to view God in this way, you will begin a walk with Him that you never dreamed possible. You will begin to view life the way He meant, with a joy He has.

As intimacy with my Father has grown deeper, my desire to bring Him into every part of my life has deepened. He has never let me down. Circumstances have let me down. Problems have let me down. People have let me down. My Father never has. He has walked by my side through physical and emotional pain.

When I take my Father into the hospital room with me, He sits by my bed and comforts me. I felt His presence through each surgery I have had. Scars remind me that even deep cuts do eventually heal. When my Father made me, he placed in my body a built-in repair system. Unless I damage that through neglect, I eventually feel the results of that system. Physical scars *can* heal.

When I take my Father into the emotional hospital with me, He also sits by my bed and comforts me. The death of my first marriage took me to the emotional wound center, and He met me there. As the woman in "A Wallflower No More" Dance touched the hem of Jesus' garment and found healing, so I touched His hem daily, seeking my healing. It came. Now I can thank God, not for divorce, but for where He carried me during my recovery. He brought me to wells of His righteousness and streams of strength, and I drank daily. Most days I drank like one who felt she had to store up His living water, like one who thought this water would soon be taken away. I sat at His table of life and stuffed myself with His bread. I went to the Scriptures to find help. I found it. He placed inside of me the ability to climb back out of my pain with His help. I felt the results of His plan. Emotional scars *can* heal.

God is looking for a personal relationship with you. He knows you best. Doesn't it make sense to let go of pride, uncertainties, and anything else that blocks your relationship with God and enter into this personal relationship?

Some of you might say, "Well, I've been a Christian all my life. I believe in Jesus. I know I'm going to heaven. That's all I need." I would simply say much more is available for you. You have not yet tapped the spiritual resources God wants to hand you. Why waste another hour without seeking Him in this personal way? What have you got to lose? In truth, you have everything to gain. He has a giant pitcher with your name on it, and He wants to fill your cup to overflowing. Won't you let Him? What is stopping you?

When I was much younger, before pain rubbed off my "Not me" attitude, I did not want to discuss my problems with anyone because I didn't think I was supposed to have any problems. To admit I did was to admit my weaknesses. As a Christian, I thought I was supposed to carry pain in a book satchel on my back, closed up and away from the view of my friends and family. I thought I could never expose the pain inside. What I could not see was that when I hid my pain, I could not become real.

Somewhere along the way, I realized that God wanted His followers to be real people, not manikins or robots. He wanted His disciples to be real enough to say they were human, hungry, and hurting. Some of the first disciples reeked of fish and walked around in clothes that had not been washed in months. I decided that is where my Father wanted to take me. He wanted to take away any false smiles, false laughter, and anything else that made me think I had it all together and show me I did not have it all together. Only in recognizing my helplessness could I recognize Him.

When I went on the Emmaus Walk, a three-day spiritual journey, I felt stirrings in me that bubbled with excitement. Those who know me now would not have known me then. Even though I was shy and quiet during that Walk, Jesus was working deeper in me during those seventy-two hours. I truly went in as a caterpillar and in the years after that, I shed my skin and began to fly. Emmaus gave me that chance. Before my Emmaus experience, I would never have thought I could speak out in a discussion group, teach a Sunday School class, or lead a Bible study. On the road to Emmaus that weekend, my eyes were opened, and I felt the love of God in new and more intimate ways. I saw Jesus, and Jesus saw me.

I have been in a fast dance ever since. I think that is because I know that my life cannot go on forever, and I want to do all I can for Him before I leave this earth. I have asked Him to squeeze everything He can out of me in the time I have left; however, He has shown me that He can use me even better if I will slow down and participate in the dances He brings me.

Because I am driven, I have to purposefully look for relaxing settings, moments when I am forced to slow down. I find those moments when a friend touches my soul with her love; when I engage in enlightening conversation; when I catch someone's sense of humor, and we laugh ourselves crazy; when I read a good book or watch a movie that captivates me with a love story; when Christian music brings me out of my problems and into worship; when verses in the Bible jump off the page and minister directly to me; and most especially when someone tells me of her experiences with her Father.

Some of my richest slow-me-down experiences come to me when my Father brings a hurting person into my office. Everything about me goes into a slow dance of listening to their problems and sharing with them what the Spirit tells me. I love giving others a chance to unload. He has taken me through so many dances with Him that I want to offer His dances to those who come to see me. My heart's desire is to help others know the power of His love, the joy of intimacy with Him. When women are crying, I want them to know He is the God who rocks them with pleasure. When they are hurting from emotional abuse, I want them to smell the corsage He pins on them. When they struggle underneath a load of heavy burdens, I want them to know that He will take those burdens. I want them to feel the green pastures of rest under their feet. I long for the moonlight of His grace to change their hearts of worry into hearts of trust. I want them to realize that desert experiences never happen in closed rooms. No matter how tough the battle, He places a door of Hope so you can leave that room.

When life became so hard for me through divorce, I knew I did not have the strength to make it on my own. I was crumbling. I had two sons who needed me, so I began to find my help in the timeless words of Scripture. I knew there had to be answers for me there.

One day I was reading Romans 8: 38-39, in which Paul tells us that there is nothing that can separate us from God's love. Those words, which I had read before, suddenly jumped off the page and into my heart. They became personal. That had never happened to me before. That's when I started realizing that Scripture is meant to bring personal discoveries, that Scripture verses are personal love letters from our Father to us. Everything in me began to vibrate with this new knowledge, as if the words from Romans 8 sat on every nerve, every muscle, every bone, and every tissue in my body. Together the words sang into my soul a love song that sounded something like this: "Others may leave. I won't. Others may find someone else. I won't. Others may view you as not as good. I won't. Others may neglect you. I won't." Romans 8: 38-39 became my lifeboat. The message felt so good. I have never stopped believing in its promise since that day so many years ago.

The discovery of God's desire to send love messages to me led to another discovery. I had heard of the Holy Spirit's power in the lives of others. I did not understand. What I had heard was challenging. I wasn't sure I wanted the Holy Spirit's power if He would make me uncomfortable. Okay, I'll be truthful. I did not want to be walking down the street and suddenly start jumping, screaming, and shouting hallelujah! I was afraid of what His power would do. In retrospect, that was ludicrous. Being the gentleman He is, He would expand Himself in me only when I invited Him to do so. He would not take control of me in any way that made me uncomfortable. Once that was settled, I felt comfortable enough to ask Him to move throughout all of my life. I felt safe with someone who would always be a gentleman. I respect the gentleman in Him. He respects the lady in me. This understanding freed me to seek the baptism of Jesus, the baptism of the Holy Spirit that John the Baptist spoke of. "I baptize you with water, but He will baptize you with the Holy Spirit." (Mark 1:8) Now, talk about a glorious experience! That is certainly one!

My journey into a deeper walk with Him has not been one in which I always stayed on the mountaintop. The most humbling experience I have ever had came from my Father God. When my young husband left me, I was talking to the Father about my ex husband's faults. Clearly I heard "You are a pilgrim, too." Those words knocked me to my knees—-literally. I repented of the thought that I was better than he was. I learned that day that anything my ex-husband had ever done I am capable of doing. His pilgrimage is between his Father and him. Plenty of things to work on exist in my own pilgrimage.

One of the best times of intimacy with my Father was the night He helped me get through the death of my mother. I know now that she stayed here as long as she could because she did not want to leave her two girls. We both adored her. At 94, nothing was wrong with her body medically. She was just tired. Her body was so frail, and on the afternoon before she died, I walked into the nursing home right after Hospice had arrived. The nurse began to tell me things I had dreaded hearing. I could not give up my mother. I didn't think I could make it on this earth without my hero.

When the nurse told me she was going to give my mother morphine to keep her from hurting as her body shut down, I could not stop crying. Suddenly, without any prior thought, I jumped up from the chair in her room and went to her side. She was practically deaf without her hearing aids. I got close to her ear and started saying *The Lord's Prayer*. She joined in. We said the *Twenty-third Psalm* together. She was so brave, but I shed enough tears for both of us. I surprised myself when I looked into her eyes and told her it was okay for her to go Home now, to see daddy and Jesus and her other family members. I sat back down and begged God for mercy for my mother. I've never begged God for anything, but I did not want my mother to go through the pain of her body shutting down.

I was home when she died two hours later. I wish I had known; I would have stayed. The nurse had said she had a week to a week and a half. Never having experienced the power of release that comes when one family member tells another that it is okay to leave, I never thought her death would happen that soon. When I got the call from my sister, I raised my hand and thanked the Lord for His mercy. I moved all over my home in a song of praise that Mother was now Home.

In an instant, I could almost see His face, and what I saw was a big smile. I have never felt so close to my Father as I did the night my mother went to Him. As I said "Thank you for mercy" to Him, I heard in my spirit "I love to give mercy. That's what I do."

That night was such a real experience that I have thought many times, "I need to call Mama and talk with her about that night. Wasn't that something the way our Father showed mercy and took you on Home? Wasn't it beautiful when we prayed together that last time?" For an instant, I forget I can't do that.

This is the intimacy I believe God wants with His children. This is the intimacy that is available through a personal relationship with your Father. This is the intimacy available as you move onto the Dance Floor of Life with your Father. Won't you meet Him there?

Printed in the United States
117286LV00001B/22-117/P